# But, Hey! What's in Your Mind & Heart Matters

DR. SOFIA LAURDEN-DAVIS
ADAMS

# Dedication

This book is titled "But, HEY! What Matters Is What's In Your Heart & Minds" is dedicated to people who have the mentality of helping the lost in this generation. To those people who have the ability to guide our children of today in the right direction. I dedicate this book to all who have the courage, and share their experiences towards positivity, and productivity and identifying the right and wrong directions to move forward in this world of chaos and confusing world. Guiding our children to the right path for them to move forward with confidence and faith heading to the right road of life.

# Contents

# INTRODUCTION

Every time I hear the song *"Coats Of Many Color"* by Dolly Parton, I feel at ease as my imagination goes through many hassles and buzzles when my son was very young age was still in high school. He was attending church with his girlfriend. He was discriminated against because of his skin color. He is my son with a Filipino father who was my husband now an ex-husband. My son now is a medical doctor. This area where we settled in 2004 is a very secluded place, which I call the boondocks. We came from New Jersey and moved to Florida in 2004, a very unpopular hidden town at that time. Another song that I am attached to the first I heard was the song titled *"Why Can't We Live Together"* by Sade.

This song of Sade is meaningful to a point where each and every one of us, since Covid lived in isolation. Not only that the culture discrimination in the country become so obvious and wide open and then on the other side, but we also turned on our mentality that everyone should be accepted. Such influences ruin our young children of today and their lives in the future. Many other lifestyles do not make sense, and that common sense is left out within our society of today.

Also, advertising such activities and practices that would

ruin human beings is now acceptable. However, may I ask you, is skin color a practice and or lifestyle of choice? Well, unless you dye your skin white, blue, brown, or black. Is skin color a disease? However, your DNA is still what you are of skin colored person. We are the children of God, and we are in many different skin color that is meant to be. However, the lifestyle and practices that ruins humans are not from God's intention, but it is human's intentions such as transgenderism lifestyle and practices is now acceptable according to an article I have read, the trans disease is a disease (Manetex 2023, Google).

Well, a boy having XYY genetic and a girl having XXX must be a disease having these 3 or 4 genomes within for a child to be born that way. Which is still a scientific process on how to cure this disease of transgenderism. A syndrome called **Androgen Insensitivity Syndrome** causes patients to **have a female shape but carry a male chromosome**. However, according to scientists, information about the state of the ancient woman is not enough to confirm this is the cause of this strange characteristic. Although there is no evidence of a woman's behavior or figure, from burial items in the grave, it can be seen that the girl is accepted and even revered by the community.

These phenomena are very much misunderstood by most of us, such as skin color discrimination and mixed cultures. Skin color and cultures are determined by DNA and RNA, or shall I say, genetically formed, and they are not diseases. You can't change that, and it is not a practiced lifestyle, it is meant to be. The normal and healthy genes for boys and girls are the genetic forms of XX for a girl, and XY for a boy.

However, for now, let us focus on understanding who we are and why each one of us has a different skin color. The Lord has given us all we need here on earth of abundance. A man and a woman are born temporarily to journey in life in this world, and we have already been provided with all we need. If there is any added genome mixed with these XX and XY, it is considered a disease. A disease can be cured, and scientists are now actively searching for the real causes of these types of diseases in humans. Where they came from, and why a pregnant woman carries a baby that has a sex disease.

So, again, skin color and mixed culture are meant to be. Practices and lifestyle choices created by humans and chosen by an individual could damage and ruin their lives later on. Most practices and lifestyles are not God's given privileges but human creation and become destructive later in life. Some of these practices I call mentally disturbed, meaning confused. Additionally, the people, media, and society's influences around these individuals since growing up also shape what our children would become.

There are practices and lifestyles that humans practice that create positive and healthy results. These will be mentioned later in this chapter. The practices and lifestyles humans develop in life can also be a learning process. However, it depends on whether an individual would change wrong practices and make them right gearing towards positive and good productivity and its results. An individual must acknowledge that some practices do not make sense and only ruin them. We hope that this individual will not slip into the pit of misery. Therefore, society should help these individuals by sharing the right way of life, if they know what the right way is. Also, guide them toward curing the disease, but not playing with it to become a practice of transgenderism, such as changing the sex organ from a boy to a girl or a girl to a boy. In similarity to having a disease, you look for a cure, not leave it or play with it until you ruin yourself, and others. An individual becomes a mentally disturbed category.

Why did I say mentally disturbed? Because there are choices in life that are chosen by an individual due to many confusions and disturbances of the mind. The Thought Universe is vast and vague, and humans can only occupy a few choices in life. To incorporate within as a lifestyle and practices in this world of plenty to be a person of who we are born as a man, or a woman. Changing the XY and XX genomes and making it a lifestyle and practices that ruin individuals, such as transgenderism causes more chaos in a child's life. A child sees and witnesses an individual who is maybe their loved one or friends from school doing and practicing transgenderism which is one of those many bad influences on our children yesterday and today. Being ourselves as humans' means being created by the LORD who completed us with his guidance and provided us with everything, we need in life here on earth. The downside of humanity is that humans want more, and therefore we gear ourselves in the wrong direction while we are journeying on earth which the Lord has already provided for us. Then we get lost due to many wrong influences and confusion begins. Therefore, humans choose the wrong direction instead of God's Master Plan for all of humanity.

Mental disturbance is due to confusion about who we really are, the Self-Universe. Based on my study and research, I must delve into the Thought Universe of each one of us to understand the human mind of the intelligence  things on earth with two major universes one of the living things on earth, the thought; and the physical universe. Let us start with why there are so many different cultural marriages that affect the mixture of each one of us, affecting our DNA and RNA.

"The world is a dangerous place to live, not because of the people who are evil, but because of the people who don't do anything about it." (Albert Einstein, Theoretical Physicist 1879-1955).

# CHAPTER 1
# Culture Mixed Marriages

A long time ago, if you were Asian. you could not marry a white human being. If you were a white man and married an Asian woman, you would be punished. Just like what happened more than 90 years ago, their belief was that mixed culture marriages were not practiced. We may say we are now in the 21st Century. Are we still carrying this type of belief? Let us find out if this type of rule still exists from a long, long time ago to today, or perhaps within us, has still not changed due to what we learned from our ancestors. We must wake up and open our minds to other chapters of our lives here on earth, which is only a temporary walk of life.

Mixed marriage was not approved in those eras before we were born on this earth. You would get in trouble for marrying another kind of race, such as Asian, Black, or White. I was and I am married to a white man with green eyes and a long nose. We have stayed together as a married couple since 1998 to 2020. If I had taken this action in those eras, I would have been hanged, and my white husband would have been hanged too. When my husband, whom I married in 1998, passed away in December 2020, I met another man, He is also white, with blue eyes, 6th feet tall, and long nose, and I agreed to marry him in November 2022. I am a Filipina with brown skin a 4'11 feet tall. I now understand that skin color does not matter at all. Again, these white men I married would have gotten in trouble for marrying an Asian woman in those eras, and too would have been hanged.

Today is different. I do believe that most understand that skin color does not matter at all. Meaning, do not judge or assume about a person through skin color. I said most understand, not all humans understand this type of mental puzzle in life that we encounter here on earth. What matters is what's in your mind; and your type of lifestyle that affects your thinking, positivity, creativity, and productivity in life. What matters is the right way to go forward in life with good and healthy results. At least you try and try again, then you become the winner of your positive action. It is very important to have what the Lord has given to all humanity, good common sense, wisdom, and good consciences. However, seared consciences, wisdom, and common sense may not understand what the right choices are due to a disturbed growing-up living style from people around us.

Previous generations, like my parents were born in the 1920s, high school education was the highest level of education attained. In today's generation, education to the highest level often aims for a doctoral degree, such a Doctor of Philosophy (PhD). Despite my father having only a high school education and my mother graduated from an intermediate level; she became a beautician. Education was always a motivating factor for my parents to improve. However, they faced financial challenges after my father suffered a stroke, causing his photography business to decline. He was unable to operate the business, and my mother's beauty parlor salon business also suffered as our lives disintegrated due to my father's illness.

Today, humans are among the most educated living beings on earth, especially in the 21st century, where education is the primary pursuit for dedicated individuals. Reflecting on those earlier eras, we can understand the discriminations based on skin color, and restrictions on marrying individuals of different races and cultures. Additionally, the ability to safely travel to other countries for pursuing personal aspirations in our temporary journey on earth involves gathering knowledge about diverse cultures and beliefs. This enables us to choose positivity, creativity, and productivity to enrich our thought universe making informed decisions using good common sense, a good conscience, and good wisdom.

As my mind imagined where America was based on my father's stories, it became a reality within my thought universe. I pondered where America is today. Although I sometimes forget during the ongoing journey on earth, there is always a reminder within my mind to come to America. For instance, when I was living in Manila in the 1970s a man was with asked if I wanted to go to the United States of America. This question has illuminated my mind since I was ten years old, when my father said I am going to America after I shared my dream with him. Even these days, I always say "Words are powerful" because our thought universe is vast, allowing us to retain information heard from influential people around us while growing up.

The words that came from my father's mouth entered my brain and stayed there for years until I grew up and remembered the word "America." At that time, when my father told me I was going to America, I innocently asked him a puzzling question wondering if America is my godmother. My father immediately responded, "America is Heaven, and you are going there in the near future." My eyes lit up, and I pondered where I was headed as grew up. So many questions filled my mind, such as where and what is America. As I envisioned what my father said- that America is heaven I pictured and saw images in my mind of angels in America. It was amazing to hear that from my father when I was young describing America as a rich country. He added that there were no poor and hungry people in America, and there was no crime explaining that America is heaven. People living in America are kind and wealthy. I innocently stored that information in my mind, and it has stayed with me for more than 60 years. Until now, I have written about it and still remember.

Again, while shaping our thought universe, or shall I say our mind, based on what we hear and learn while growing up from influential people around us, we become that person. All the words that come from the mouths of people around us shape who we are while growing up; and who we may become. We learn from what we hear from others around us. Without utilizing our God given talents, such as good common sense, good consciences, and good wisdom, we become  victims of forming ourselves heading in the wrong direction of life as we journey on this earth of plenty.

Due to my father's story about my dream when I was 10 years old, I decided to educate myself, seeking more knowledge about many different cultures in the world. My curiosity about cultures in America led me to study Liberal Arts and Photography 1992, back in New Jersey from Hawaii. In 1996, I focused on Social Behavior, Arts, Cultures, American History, and legendary people who came to America at the beginning of Americans living in this land of plenty. I found out that America, or shall we call the "United States of America" (USA), has mixed cultures originating from many different countries worldwide.

My experiences as a naïve foreign-born girl living on American soil for more than 39 years, led me to want to know more about the life of Americans, on the other side of what my father had said. I was still puzzled by his description of America as rich, with its people being angels, white, and kind. I then became a volunteer for the Guardian Ad Litem Program and visited families and children who were neglected and abused.  Through this, I encountered many struggling white individuals and children with

But, Hey! What's in Your Mind & Heart Matters

blond hair facing hunger and abandonment.

# CHAPTER 2

# What Matter Is What's In The Mind And Heart

Whether your skin color is white, brown, yellow, or black, it does not matter. What matters is who we are within-the content of our hearts and minds as individual persons--not your skin color. To move forward in our life pursuits and lifestyles, we must choose what is right on our journey in life. We are just temporary residents here on this earth of plenty, and we are blessed with freedom. However, in this world full of choices, we must ensure that we choose the right direction with God's guidance and be thankful for all the blessings we receive every day.

In the book titled "Be Still and Know" by Broad Street Publishing, (2016, page 341) *"Do not conform to the pattern of this world but be transformed by the renewing of your mind. Then you will be able to test and approve what God's will is—his good, pleasing and perfect will."* The prayer says, *"Thank you, father for the changes you are making in life, I enjoy being transformed by you, polished like the silver brought out for special occasions."* (Romans 12:2 NIV).

I am so thankful that I met those angels when I came to America in the year 1984 as one of the Chinese hired workers at

World Expo 84 in New Orleans. I am here on American soil, and undoubtedly, I am blessed. I pray every day and am always thankful for what I have on this earth of plenty. I was able to continue my education here in America, which has been my goal since I was young, I am now a doctor, holding a PhD in Human Services, Management, and Leadership. I continue my pursuit to move forward.

As I have explained in my book that just got published titled *"The Memoir: The River of Life,* I am thankful to the Lord for what I have learned, and I know how to adjust myself for any type of life issues, hardship in life, and struggles.

Until these days, I unconsciously gravitate towards the colors red and gray, I buy gray colored dresses, my wedding dress was silver-gray, and the cabana door and walls are based on red and gray, reminiscent of the color of the airplane I dreamt of when I was 10 years old.

Currently, I write this book, I am in the process of renovating my parents' house that was ruined by Typhoon Odette in the Philippines. The wall color will be gray, and the doors will be red mirroring the choices I made for my recently sold cabana, similarly choosing my wedding clothes of red and silver, gray color. This ideas was influenced by my father and my dream has carried  from my childhood; to my 60s.

The main point is that the influential people around us during our formative years shape who we are become. Despite the many struggles I have encountered, I am thankful for the positive influences in my life since childhood.

The name "America is Heaven" is ingrained in my mind, and I continue to share stories about it to everyone. I remember those memories and what my father told me. Analyzing the concept of "heaven." in my own version, it represents a place of successes and how we live on this earth of plenty. From a young age, I was already ingrained with the idea of being an entrepreneur.

My mother was also influential in my life. As a child, I used to accompany her to buy fish in the ocean fishermen who were wholesalers. We would then sell the fish to our neighborhood. The basket would be full of bubbling anchovies and water from the basket would drop onto my hair and clothes. When I returned from selling fish, my mother would advise me to change my wet clothes, to avoid getting sick. She would count the money give me my salary, and that became the money I saved. This early experience influenced my personality and instilled in me the drive to earn income. Thanks to the influence my parents, I became a businesswoman, an entrepreneur as detailed in my book titled, "Entrepreneurial Minds: To Branch out through Experiences and Education. This book narrates the story that brought me to where I am today as a self-employed individual.

Although I am a 66-year-old woman, I still exhibit childlike behavior, finding joy in laughter and enjoying life wherever I am. I appreciate what the Lord has given to all humanity, and you may be surprised that we already have everything in life. We must see and look through our own senses, good common sense, and good wisdom, carrying the good consciences that the Lord has bestowed upon all humans here on this earth of plenty; then, we are truly in heaven.

That's my interpretation of heaven. In my other I recently published book titled "The Two Universes of Self" the Thought Universe is vast and vague, while the Physic Universe involves visible actions that all humanity can see. The unseen universe, the Thought Universe contains so many choices that cannot be seen. It depends on your choices in life--the Physic Universe acts visually, and the results affect the Self-Universe. So, what are your choices in life?

What is within us can cause devastation and prosperity in life. Therefore, you must know the difference between your choices and actions. We must distinguish the meanings of different words, such as boastfulness and pride. Pride can be good or bad depending on how we use it. I share a story of a couple where the husband has pride in being, as we say, "a man" "believing he should not be asking his wife for anything because he knows better than her. This traditional belief ruined part of the couple's togetherness. Partners in life whether husband and wife, should have a balanced life just like the yin-yang in the Chinese symbol of balance. Wrong pride can cause destruction in life. Weaknesses and strengths of both husband and wife must be utilized for their relationship to be strong.

I then became one of the survivors living in this world of plenty a mix of darkness and light. Examples of the familiar "concept of ""survival of the fittest" persist to this generation where imperialistic thoughts based on skin colors still make a difference that continues to exist. Another example is prosperity and opportunities among humanity are often still based on skin color. We must backtrack and delve into the history of where each one of us came from considering the white, black, brown, yellow, and red skin colors.

Being born and living in the United States for a decade, ancestral knowledge may be forgotten; and left behind. In schools, the subject of Ancestry might be removed due to confusion, possibly thinking it is a form of discrimination. But why do we base judgments on skin color when understanding a person's capabilities and who they are deep inside. Why? Is this discrimination still present today? Instead of focusing on skin color, job application often inquiries about it. Why not ask questions related to citizenship, knowledge, skills, and applicant's capabilities? Similarly, questions in hospitals or doctor's clinics now preferences about sexual activity.

In making a generalization about every human on this issue, society seems to be more accepting of alternative choices in sexual relationships, like those between men or women. However, there is still disagreement and discrimination based on skin color. The confusion deepens when considering the traditional view of a man and a woman being married, known as husband and wife. This world has become perplexing., and the distinctions between right and wrong are increasingly unclear. It seems we are not applying good common sense, good wisdom, and good consciences in navigating these complexities. In this book you will see Albert Einstein theorical passage such as *"The world is a dangerous place to live, not because of the people who are evil, but because of the people who don't do anything about it"* (Albert Einstein Theoretical Physicist 1879-1955).

This activity of humanity should NOT be in application for all humans because we are not, and we don't practice that lifestyle. Again, generalization of knowing a patient through questionnaires with the content that does not make sense to those who are in the right tract of life is very disturbing to people. Not only very disturbing to people who are on the right track in life, it is also a message to all that the wrongdoing of an individual is acceptable. Therefore, confusion between right and wrong for our children of today is a devastation of the mind and heart in understanding what's right and wrong practices and lifestyles. Therefore, our children of today, and some mentally dysfunctional individuals, think it is right to marry to a man if you are a man, and a woman to a woman. The questions in many Health Care Industries or clinic where you are going. *"Are you a transgender? What type of dildo you use"?* These questions have no respect for the people who are in the RIGHT TRACT of life in that regard.

Now when an individual is admitted in the hospital, the paperwork a person is filling out is *"Are you a boy, a girl, transgender, do you use dildo, what do you use for sexual activity?"* And these questions are very disgusting and reflect a very poor mentality of generalization and acceptance of practices and lifestyles of transgenderism. A questionnaire of generalizing individuals and their sexual activities through application questions in hospitals and clinics is very insulting to those people who are on the right track of life. Today's acceptable practices and lifestyles by humans who are lost in this life journey on the earth of plenty, transgenderism practices, affect the people who are on the right track of life; and the children of the next generations to follow.

It should not be generalization for all patients, and the questionnaires should show respect for people who are on the RIGHT TRACK of life. These types of questions should only be asked when they are with the doctor, a separate questionnaire in a private setting if you need to know who these patients are and what type of disease these patients have. Because not all are transgender or engage in sexual practices that involve toys or any transgender lifestyle. That is also one of the many reasons that individual practice these lifestyles thinking it is acceptable. Are there any guidelines in morality and good ethics?

America is a multicultural and diverse country, now is like the Philippines, but in some other corners of this continent, multicultural diversity is—a misunderstood and unacceptable regarding skin color. However, I have found out in the Philippines there are so many transgender practices and lifestyles. This type of practice, transgenderism, is acceptable to many. I was born in the Philippines. My husband Cameron and I visited the country where I was born, and I am seeing all these transgenderism practices. Again, transgender practices are acceptable in many countries like the USA and the Philippines, and many other countries, I assume.

Seeing all these individuals in the WRONG TRACK of life was very sad. The SADDEST part of all is this transgenderism practice and lifestyle is NOW ACCEPTABLE. Nobody is complaining about this trans disease. We somehow let it be, instead of looking for a cure. Transforming a sex organ to another is not the cure for this type of disease. Scientists are now finding what should be the cure for this type of disease, trans disease. The research should start from pregnancy, medication a woman had taken while being pregnant, and many other manipulations to sex organs that created trans disease. *"Woman don't cry for me but cry for your children"* (Bible Verse Luke 23:28-31) said Jesus while on the cross. I can now see what the Lord was saying then, and now it's here, and it's coming your way. Again, *"The world is a dangerous place to live, not because of the people who are evil, but because of the people who don't do anything about it"* (Albert Einstein Theoretical Physicist 1879-1955).

Regarding skin color, however, discrimination still exists to these days. Natural skin color of an individual is not a practice. However, coloring of the skin is a practice made up by humans. The question would be, are our children negatively affected by coloring their skin? These generations created some kind of lotion for the skin to make it white or brown color. But this change of skin color is NOT through DNA or RNA. Skin Color comes from a NATURALLY BORN individual such as through DNA and RNA of an individual is not a practice.

For instance, a population of 99 percent is unable to adapt to change in a culturalized society. Skin color is through DNA and RNA process. WE CANNOT change that. I do believe that skin color is God's creation. Trans disease is a disease. I hope that medicine, scientists, and researchers are now active in researching the cure for trans disease. I will explain that clearly in the next chapter about how trans disease exists.

Either the population is reluctant to adapt to change, and the reality of scientific results of any kind such as skin color, and reluctant to alter their beliefs and values or unless numb to knowledge that there are countries and or most countries are now a globalized world and are changing rapidly. Again, in SKIN COLOR, we as humans cannot change that. Now, I found out while on vacation in the country where I was born transgenderism practice and lifestyle are acceptable. I encountered these individuals, and as a writer, I have the right and freedom to express my thinking about humans' practices in life that I know will ruin them in the near future.

I DO NOT accept these transgenderism practices. I was very ashamed, and I felt sad for these individuals who practice this type of lifestyle, transgenderism. My philosophical view may not be accepted by many. However, in this world of many life choices, we must select the best for ourselves and of our children for today and tomorrow. Select the right way that benefits all humans. We do not want to gear our children in the wrong direction in life. Let me give you an example of society who closes their mouths to give and share the knowledge of what is supposed to be the right thing to do. Because the right thing with good common sense, good conscience, and good wisdom to do is NOT recognized anymore these days. Let me give you a few examples.

In April 2006, my first colloquia experience was interesting because I was with my core group for a panel discussion and within this room, there were 20 tables, and the room was walled all the way around. The blockage of the room around created echoes from our voices in the entire room. When loudly talking, each table member cannot hear each other's conversation. In my table, we were debating who would go to the next table to tell them to lower their voices down. There were no volunteers. Most of the members were reluctant to tell the other table to lower their voice, so we were all able to hear each other's conversation. Then I volunteered. But first, let us comment on what my panelists said before I volunteered. "No, we can't say any comment concerning this issue" they said! "No, that is rude, and you cannot stop people talking loudly." Why? I asked. It is not rude to ask them to lower down their voice, I said to the panelist at our table.

Therefore, I walked to the next table and asked them to lower down their voices so that we could hear each other on the other table. Their answers were "Yes, we can't hear each other either. Thank you for telling us." They also had the same problem! So, my point of view was that why they were afraid to confront people if they were a nuisance? Why are we afraid to tell an individual who practices transgenderism if we know that this practice and lifestyle, transgenderism, will create havoc in their lives in the future? So, why can't we say something? I do believe that humans are so confused about what's right and what's wrong to say, and that is the saddest part of humanity. Einstein said: *"The world is a dangerous place to live, not because of the people who are evil, but because of the people who don't do anything about it"* (Einstein, 1879-1955).

Continuing my Doctor of Philosophy (PhD) major in Human Services at Capella University, Colloquia is part of the Scholar's activity as a researcher. In April 2008, Colloquia in Atlanta I learned that social research is free society but at the same time, Positivism controls Pragmatism in social science. At my table, I was not aware that one of the people there was the professor responsible for guiding us in choosing a dissertation topic. She did not introduce herself, and therefore, I thought that we were all students at the table.

I have a habit if no one says something, am responsible for saying something. I am always the one to open my mouth to move on. The professor spoke out but somehow asked questions about what we were going to do for that day. I spoke out and shared my ideas on what we needed to talk about. As I said, if no one would say something, I feel obligated to speak up. However, this professor did not come back the next day, and we were assigned another professor. Somehow, no one would sit at our table.

Until this day, I am still puzzled if I am the cause of these many incidents. I prayed to the Lord to guide me not ignore the right thing to say and do, but instead, to share it because many of us are now lost in the jungle of Good Manners and Right Conduct. I may say that all of us may already be contaminated steering our lifestyles in the wrong directions because no one cares anymore. In this new generation, we are so blinded by what's right and wrong.

Therefore, I study myself on how to react to other people while in a group like these. That is why this writing of mine exists. The main point of this passage is that most of us do not know what's right and wrong to say anymore. For example, we cannot criticize the wrong practices of transgenderism (human's creation) because of the fear that we are criticizing them, but the criticism of skin color still exists, which is God's creation, or shall I say the frisky hair of a person with dark skin, which is a natural born trait, and it comes from the DNA and or RNA. But the ABNORMAL practice such as transgenderism, WE DON'T say anything about this wrongdoing of an individual! Why? I am so puzzled with humanity not knowing what's right and wrong anymore!

On June 16, 2008, I had a Guardian Ad Litem Program (GALP) training started in June 16 through June 24 of 2008. There were five attendees at the GAL training. In the second day, as soon as I commented about one volunteer said about religion that we cannot stretch to advocate a child which against the law policy, and only we could gear them towards religion if the client chose to but not with our own initiative. I agree. Therefore, I clarify that as GALP volunteers we are impartial to the case, and religion is also the same. After my expression the next day the volunteer trainee did not come. I was wondering if I said something wrong. The next 4th day goal

But, Hey! What's in Your Mind & Heart Matters

was cultural diversity.

One volunteer trainee said that she was learning how African American comb their hair. *"The secret of it all is on how to calm down their hair is to calm down themselves, then their hair should be calm also, instead of becoming friskier every time they are stressed out"*. The volunteer was talking about the girl's frisky hair (1st Panelist). In the classroom, another volunteer commented that adopting a child should only be within their own racial group. She said the causes of adapting to a different race would be devastating to a child. For instance, African American to only African American, White children to only white people. Another volunteer also commented about white people. She said, *"why is that there are white people only adapting black children"* (2nd panelist). I commented that besides acculturation process in the community this is our opportunity to learn other cultures by adopting children from another race. Another volunteer disagreed and the next day, she did not come back to the training.

Again, SKIN COLOR is not a practice or lifestyle. Skin color is through DNA and RNA we cannot change that and that is GOD's CREATION. However, transgenderism such as XYY for boys and for a girl is XXX the sexual organ has a disease. The definition of transgender is "relating *to, or being a person, whose gender identity differs from the sex the person was identified as having birth especially... of relating to or being a person, whose gender identity is opposite the sex the person was identified as having at birth*" (Webster Dictionary). According to Einstein, the world is a dangerous place to live, not because of the people who are evil, but because of the people who don't do anything about it" (Albert Einstein Theoretical Physicist 1879-1955)

# CHAPTER 3

# The Consequences Of Immorality Practices & Lifestyles

A long time ago, or perhaps it continues in today's generation, but it is hidden underground, shall I say? Why did transgenderism become the practice of previous generations and continue to the present day? First, let me share what I know as a researcher and a Doctor of Philosophy. I have encountered many articles about this issue. In the previous generation, the baby boomer era and before, it was mandatory to have a baby boy because these generations needed a man for farming, heavy tasks, and many other reasons that required a male presence. Therefore, if a fetus was identified as a baby girl, parents would change the sex organs to make it a baby boy. That was the practice in the past. My question is, does this practice still exist today but remain hidden? However, the XY chromosome for a boy and XX for a girl cannot be changed unless a child undergoes an operation. In those eras, there was no available research on the genome of a baby.

First, let us learn about X and Y chromosomes. Chromosome XX denotes a female, and Chromosome XY denotes a male. "If the sperm that fertilizes an egg has an X chromosome, the baby is female; if it has a Y chromosome, the baby will be a boy" (Google,

2023). However, all eggs produced by the female have an X sex chromosome, and all sperm from the male have either an X or Y chromosome. If an X sperm fertilizes the egg first, you'll have a girl (XX), and if a Y sperm fertilizes the egg, you get a boy (XY) (Google, 2023). It only takes a sperm to determine the baby's sex organ.

That means, if it's a boy, it is a boy. If it's a girl, it is a girl. There is no transformation from a boy to a girl or vice versa, such as in individual transgenderism practices and lifestyles. If an individual changes their sexual identity, it is considered a disease (Google, 2023). Since an individual is challenging the natural way of life that God created, there will be consequences. If the disease is not cured, the child's life may become chaotic.

Instead of finding a cure for XYY or XXX, what are the examples of consequences later in life when an individual practices the transgenderism lifestyle and changes the sex organs? It will have a very devastating effect on your children practicing transgenderism lifestyles. Please see the list below:

1.  Suicidal thoughts and attitudes and defensive behavior.

2.  A man pretending to be a woman entering the bathrooms of women or girls, or vice versa, leading to the occurrence of rape.

3.  HIV diseases: Global data on HIV/AIDS is rising, and there

are many HIV/AIDS cases in the Philippines. There are 39 million HIV cases, 630,000 AIDS-related deaths globally, and in the Philippines alone, there have been 121,075 cases of HIV/AIDS from January 1984 to August 2023 (One News, 2023).

4.  Promiscuity leading to the ruin of marriages.

5.  Immoral practices that serve as bad influences on our children today and future generations.

6.  Taxpayers paying for sex changes, and insurance covering transgenderism-related immoralities. As a society, we contribute through health insurance, ultimately supporting all members of the insurance organization we are affiliated with.

Perhaps there are many more consequences that we are unaware of. Why does our society accept these types of immorality and dysfunctional activities of individuals that harm themselves and our present and future children? Why does society agree with the wrongdoing of these individuals? Is it because we, as a society, no longer care? Maybe we just do not know how to respond to the immorality of individuals practicing transgenderism lifestyles.

Why do these individuals practice transgenderism? Please see the list below:

1. Parents' choice for a fetus to be a boy or a girl, which was the practice decades ago and perhaps continues to these days (practices and beliefs).

2. Influences from people around these children while growing up (psychological issues).

3. For males, the release of feelings and emotions from decades ago was/is NOT acceptable (psychological issue).

4. A single mother raising a boy (influential individual imitating a mother, such as girly movements and makeup, as a woman, a psychological issue).

5. Bullies around these children (psychological issue).

6. Enforced feeling to be a boy or vice versa due to circumstances (psychological issue).

7. Inherited behavior from relatives and influenced by people around these individuals (psychological issue).

8. Alcohol and drugs to numb the pain within (psychological issue).

9. Many more occurrences that we don't even know, understanding the inside of the minds and hearts of these individuals.

Another issue in our society these days is the life of fallacy, revolving around money, publicity, and popularity. If a person has money to pay marketers or advertising companies, there are no rules of morality, common sense, and conscience. Instead, it's all about money to earn more money. Meaning, if you want to advertise yourself in a magazine or on television and radio, you can pretend and advertise whatever you want to promote your product, even if it's all untrue about your product and yourself.

It's about giving the society what it wants to hear, supporting many immoralities. In today's practices, life is a fantasy, a pretentious lifestyle. Information through magazines, advertisements, and marketing products for self-popularity if you have the money to pay these marketers. In advertising an individual to become popular, the lies beneath these goals for advertising and marketing is to promote the lies and fantasy world of a business or an individual. However, there is no truth about the product and the individual.

Furthermore, there are no complaints about these issues in our society today. People either accept it as right, or if they accept it as wrong, their reasoning is a "Not My Business" mentality. Not to mention that when you eat at a restaurant, the rules now mandate giving a 15, 18, or 20 percent tip to a waitress serving you, and some restaurants already charge 15 percent of the service fee. In the previous generation, customers were the ones to decide if the service was good, and then the waitress would be given tips. There is so much change in silence that does not make sense at all. Common sense, conscience, and wisdom are totally neglected by humans.

I have given examples here from the book titled "Be Still And Know" (Broadstreet Publishing 2016). "Bless the Lord, O my soul, and forget not all his benefits, who forgives all your iniquity, who heals all your diseases, who redeems your life from the pit, who crowns you with steadfast love and mercy, who satisfies you with good so that your youth is renewed like the eagle's" (Psalm 103:2-5 ESV).

"Is it reasonable to believe that a marathon runner can finish a race without a single replenishing cup of water? Would it be fair to expect a doctor, after working a 36-hour shift, to have the energy to perform one last tedious surgery? Can a child be expected not to lick the spatula that mixed the cookie dough? Should a foreigner be familiar with the customs of a new land?

We know that humans have limits. We need to eat and drink regularly. We get tired and cranky if we don't have enough sleep. Our emotions can be overwhelmed by life's great upheavals. Whether you are at peak performance or running on empty, needing renewal now or in the future, God alone can give you what you need because he knows your limits and capabilities. He knows that you need time to refuel, space to recover your strength, and that sometimes a little cookie dough goes a long way" (Broadstreet Publishing, 2016).

**Prayer**: "God, I need your renewal; I know that I cannot be strong forever. I need you to replenish my energy, renew my mind, and give me strength" (Broadstreet Publishing, page 349, 2016).

The subtitle of the passage is "Ancient Paths," and it says: "Stand at the crossroads and look; ask for the ancient paths, ask where the good way is, and walk in it, and you will find rest for your souls" (Jeremiah 6:16 NIV).

"It's fun to get something new—especially if you are a technician who loves gadgets. The long lines at Apple stores around the country prove that most of us are enamored with the latest and greatest. We don't like being outdated or not living on the cutting edge.

At times we can feel a bit outdated in our spiritual lives and need a refreshing touch from God. We may need reviving, but in the kingdom of God, old is better. In fact, ancient is best! In our church, worship styles change, programs and methods too, but one thing must remain old, and that is the truth of God's Word. The old-time religion is still what rescues people from perishing. Since there is no need to update the gospel, perhaps what we need is just a fresh anointing of the Holy Spirit to fill us with contentment and rest for our souls" (Broadway Publishing 2016).

**Let us pray**: "Heavenly Father, I am in need today of a touch from you. My spirit feels dry and outdated, and my soul needs refreshment. I want to follow your ancient paths where the good way is, so give me a fresh beginning this day!" (Broadstreet Publishing, page 364, 2016).

As mentioned previously, humans often ignore and forget good common sense, wisdom, and a good conscience. We must use these skills given by the Lord because they are the tools for humans to distinguish between right and wrong. However, if these mentioned skills have already been seared, then they are no longer usable. If your common sense is no longer functioning, you become a victim of immorality and the world's wrongdoing. Einstein says, "The world is a dangerous place to live, not because of the people who are evil, but because of the people who don't do anything about it" (Albert Einstein, Theoretical Physicist 1879-1955).

# CHAPTER 4

# Where Do We, Humans Came From

I couldn't find the best title for this book, but I chose the title "Hey!" to grab the attention of all humanity. Let me give you an example of where I came from. Each of us comes from many different races, places, countries, and cultures, creating a mixed culture. For instance, I am a Filipina, born in the Philippines, which is now an independent nation. However, the Philippines, with 7,600 islands, 120 to 187 languages, and more than 170 dialects, exists and is becoming a popular destination for travelers (Google, 2023).

The Philippines was occupied by the Spaniards and settled for 333 years. Discussing other Spanish countries such as Puerto Rico, Panama, and those with similar Spanish-speaking languages may have faced a situation similar to the Philippine Islands. Spaniards, as you can imagine, occupied many nations that later became independent. Today, Spain is a nation settled in Europe. Recently, I've heard of the American and Philippines governments coming together to improve the Philippines Islands.

In this book, I would like to focus on the faces of many Americans today. I aim to illustrate how they look, not fitting the traditional definition of White Americans but rather as the results of Europe's occupying nation activities many decades ago. Due to global migrations since before Columbus's time, we all appear alike, regardless of our skin color—whether white, black, tan, red, or yellow. Distinguishing people based on their skin colors is inappropriate due to ongoing global migrations. According to many writers, particularly about Asian women, especially Filipina women, they are migrant workers, but we seem naïve about global migration.

According to Hawthorne, most migrated workers from Asia are women, with 83 percent being Filipina women. These skilled women are often invisible and unrecognized. Their economic and social contributions were considered trivial or nonexistent because migrating women were routinely viewed as dependents of male migrants or as passive participants in migration (Hawthorne, 2001, p.213). Today, the initial assumption often revolves around whether a Filipina was married to an American soldier and brought to America.

My experiences share some similarities with those who faced stereotypes in World War II. While some may view Filipina women as marrying American men to escape poverty in the Philippines, my situation differs. I am not married to an American to escape poverty, and I am not married to a white American soldier for my journey to America.

Hawthorne continued, stating that Filipina women, skilled workers, came to America to find work due to overspending on education in the Philippines. The demand for workers in the U.S. and the Middle East healthcare industry forced the trend of female nurses' migration. In the Philippines, 2.3 million jobs were created, and 3.5 million Filipinos entered the workforce. The legitimate reason for deteriorating salaries in their country led to 277,000 unemployed college graduates and 700,000 documented Filipino workers leaving to work overseas.

In total, 5.7 million Filipinos joined the stock of documented workers, with some in 160 countries around the world. Asian migrant workers are expected to speak English for qualification. There are some who could not pass the test for some reasons such as pronunciation of the word "_hyper_tension" pronounce it as "_hypo_tension" which may be the reason applicant can be disqualified from employment. When this happens, they are forced to take temporary low-paying jobs such as domestic helpers or nannies. Their goal is to earn income, although low, it is sufficient to pay what they owe back home (Hawthorne, 2001).

Jung's article (1995) emphasizes the significance of War Brides and the discrimination faced by Filipinos during the years when Filipino-American soldiers fought in the war. In World War II, it was a common practice for Filipino American U.S. soldiers to marry young Filipina women. At that time, in the Bay Area of California, there were 261,273 people of Filipino ancestry, which is the second-largest concentration in the United States. In 1661, the first law against interracial marriage was passed to prevent black-white marriages existing in 38 states. In 1905, these laws were extended to prohibit marriages between whites and Asians. These laws were deemed unlawful in 1948 and fully abolished in 1967. Despite all struggles, 17,660 Filipino-American U.S. soldiers were married to Filipina women (Jung, 1995).

Another article, "Mis-education of Filipino" (2000), explains the education process for Filipinos in the American way. While Americans were preparing Filipinos for self-government, the Department of Education was never entrusted to any Filipino to manage or govern. Article 23 of the Jones Act placed Americans as heads of all educational departments during the time when Filipinos were preparing to govern their own country. The Filipino education structure followed American rules and regulations, possibly persisting until today due to the widespread use of the English language in the Philippines. The goal was to shape young Filipino minds to conform to the American ideology, introducing English language, American textbooks, American heroes, and American songs. However, Filipinos in America today are often treated as strangers (p.5).

Pratt's article (1997) provides detailed information on how stereotypes of Filipina women were integrated. The stereotypes discussed in Pratt's article are from Vancouver, Canada, and British Columbia. The research involved interviews with domestic helpers, nanny agencies, and clients, revealing inconsistencies and contradictory attitudes and feelings among the interviewees.

According to Pratt (1997), one result of the research process stated that Filipina women are perceived as both uncivilized and poorly motivated, as well as well-educated. These ambivalences are interpreted in terms of anxieties about maternal substitution, colonial pasts, racial differences, and working mothers. Some implications of the inconsistency in agents' portrayals of Filipina nannies for political practices are briefly outlined. Vancouver, Canada, British Columbia, and America share similarities in stereotypes toward Filipina women workers.

As a Doctor of Philosophy (PhD), my philosophical view and question would be: if Filipinos were taught and acculturated by Americans, how then did Filipina women become perceived as uncivilized and poorly motivated, yet somehow well-educated? The three words, uncivilized, poorly motivated, and well-educated, do not seem to align. Although Filipina women are well-educated, Pratt also questions the phenomena concerning Filipina women categorized as domestic workers, nannies, housekeepers, being perceived as uncivilized and childlike.

Another article I had reviewed was an article authored by Bautista (2002) titled: *Manilaman: The Filipino Roots in America.* The first Filipino settlement in Louisiana bayous was in the year

1763. "The year was 1763, and the schooner had unloaded its cargo at the Spanish provincial capital of New Orleans. Then its crew of Filipino sailors jumped ship and fled into the nearby cypress swamp..." (p.5). In Coloma's article (2006), the first Filipino settlement is dated back to the year 1587 in Moro Bay, California, with similar reasons for jumping ship from the Spanish galleon trade (p.4).

Perhaps, the historical name-calling for Filipino people continues to this day. The name-calling of Filipino people as savages, childlike, domestic helpers, nannies, and unmotivated originates from the 1945 World War II context. Additionally, many still believe that Filipina women are in America primarily because they married American soldiers then and now. Due to the Filipino colonialism phenomena, especially Filipina women, are called savages, childlike, and unmotivated individuals in Vancouver, Canada, British Columbia, and the United States.

Although Filipinos are known today as well-educated individuals, it contradicts the stereotypes labeling them as savages, childlike, domestic helpers, nannies, and unmotivated individuals. These widespread phenomena affect Asian Americans, Filipino Americans, or AAPI in America and other countries.

I must also mention that there is confusion about people from India, which is a different culture, not Filipinos. India has its own country, and Filipinos are in the Philippines. Another misunderstanding involves Native Americans, who are not Indians from India. Native Americans live in American soils, and we refer to them as Native Americans.

Human activities around the world, such as the first humans' travels, continue today. If countries like America and Canada do not incorporate cultural history into their school curricula, ignorance persists, leading to misunderstandings about Filipino culture.

Today, the Philippines has become the best tourism country in the world. I have witnessed this firsthand. My husband and I visited the Philippines, where I was born, exploring places like Palawan, Cebu, Bohol, Manila, and many other cities that are now tourist spots worldwide. Filipinos working in other countries often come back to invest in their hometowns in the Philippines. The Philippines is now a tourist destination for people from every country, as I observed in 1991, 2011, and 2023. The term "Balikbayan" refers to a born Filipino who worked abroad and returned to their home country, the Philippines.

You know where I am going with this section of the book. Let me ask you a question. Where are you coming from? Aren't you some kind of mixed culture? All of us in this world have mixed cultures. Do not be surprised because we are all mixed – Europeans, Spaniards, Japanese, Chinese, Mexicans, Americans, Filipinos, and many other countries not mentioned here. Ask yourself where your ancestry came from. In fact, my next books to be published soon will be "The Lost Civilization of the Davis'" and "The Lost Civilization of the Adams."

America is a melting pot place. I have been in America for more than 40 years. My son grew up here and faced discrimination in church due to his skin color. One member opposed my son's membership because of his skin color. Although he is now a medical doctor, the experience was devastating. American mentality sometimes assumes that anyone other than white is considered an outsider. I also need to talk about education in America versus education in other countries. Individuals educated in America often have to return to their own country to apply the knowledge they gained because educated individuals from other countries are not always acknowledged or are judged by their appearances.

What do Americans look like anyway? Do we, as Americans, know how America became a melting pot for every culture around the world? I understand that we learn one thing at a time, especially if we are not studying the history of our country. But still, countries that strive to be liberal, such as the United States and the Philippines, have mixed beliefs due to teachings from ancestors and the new generation creating new lifestyles and practices. However, we are Americans or Filipinos anyway. The mixed skin color – are they Americans? The mixed culture and skin color of Filipinos – are they Filipinos? Let us go back to the beginning of the Philippines and examine who the Filipinos are. For one of many examples, let us start with the Philippines, where I was born. The Philippines is now a mix of various cultures. In many different places in Europe, Asia, and of course, America, individuals from the United States of America are moving to the Philippines with its many islands – 7,600 islands with numerous dialects, perhaps around 1,500.

Furthermore, individuals of Filipino descent have been settling in the United States since the 1500s. Filipinas came to the United States through various circumstances, not solely by marrying American soldiers or Americans through arranged marriages. Examples of these circumstances include parental petitions, contract work, documented workers, visitors, investors, students, and possibly marriages to American soldiers, resulting in children born on American soil. Similar to other cultures that are not white, stereotypes towards Filipina women in Vancouver, Canada, British Columbia, and the United States impact Asian Americans collectively. Moreover, these stereotypes are rooted in historical contexts dating back to the 1900s.

Phenomena such as depicting Filipinos as childlike, savages, and unmotivated may or may not persist among today's Filipino people. Nevertheless, stereotypes persist as if we are still living in the 1900s. The underlying logic assumes that since Filipinos were labeled as savages, childlike, and unmotivated back then, contemporary Asian Americans, unaware of their heritage, become unwitting participants in perpetuating these stereotypes. The stereotype towards Filipina women also affects all Asian women, even those unfamiliar with their own country, the Philippines.

This topic served as one of my research studies during my graduate studies, pursuing a Doctor of Philosophy in Human Services. The proposed study aimed to investigate the root causes of stereotypical phenomena. The goal was to educate society about the diverse Asian descent populations and eliminate confusion between Asian Americans, Asians, Asia Minor, Pacific Islanders, Mexicans, Puerto Ricans, Spaniards, and the people of the Philippines.

Another area explored in this study was the segmentation of cultures, beliefs, economy, and motivations. For example, examining the rationales and motivations behind Filipina women marrying American soldiers and vice versa. Secondly, the study focused on the economic crisis as a priority concern for solving financial problems. Thirdly, it delved into understanding the motivations of domestic helper agencies and their clients who characterize Filipina women as childlike and unmotivated individuals. The study emphasized that generalizations based on skin color, categorizing individuals as black, white, brown, red, and green, further divide America. The proposed solution advocated addressing the issues directly rather than focusing on skin color, applicable to resolving problems in America, Canada, and British Columbia. *Skin color does not matter at all. What matters is what's in your hearts and minds. Therefore, skin color should not be the determination of who is bad or good.* It must be what's in the mind of an individual and the teachings of influential people around them that contribute to both color discrimination and the practice of changing gender. I am highlighting these two examples, skin color, and gender-changing practices due to their very different meanings, outcomes, and understandings.

These teachings and influential figures share their beliefs with their children and friends, shaping the mindset of individuals. The content of one's mind plays a crucial role in determining whether an individual aligns with these beliefs, depending on their strengths, skills, creativity, common sense, conscience, and wisdom.

Firstly, let me clarify that being transgender is a disease; it is a condition that requires understanding and acceptance of a disease to find cure. In contrast, skin color is NOT a disease; it is an inherent characteristic determined by DNA, not a lifestyle or practice.

The XX genome corresponds to a girl, and XY corresponds to a boy. If the genome deviates from this binary system, such as XYY or XXX, it can be considered a genetic disorder or illness. Diseases require a cure to address the underlying issues. While it is unclear when scientists started researching a cure for transgender experiences, ongoing research is being conducted to understand and address these concerns (Manetex, 2023).

Quoting Einstein, "The world is a dangerous place to live, not because of the people who are evil, but because of the people who don't do anything about it." Recognizing that XYY is considered a genetic disorder, efforts must be made to find a cure. This is crucial to prevent individuals from resorting to changing their sexual organs through surgery, causing harm to themselves and those around them.

# CHAPTER 5

# Is Reverse Discrimination Exists For the White Race?

I call this reverse discrimination because no one is really paying attention to the white race anymore. Perhaps, we think they are the causes of discrimination. Due to national attention to all colored people, white people have been left out regarding the needs and knowledge of the White race, as our new generations of Millennials born in 1981-1996, Generation X born in 1997-2012, Generation Alpha born in 2013-2025 need to know. The history of the White people may diminish in the next generation because of too much emphasis and focus on colored people. Not because my husband is white, it must have something to do with it; again, "common sense" is not used. Colored people are the priority regarding emphasis on crime, poverty, neglect, abuse, needs, substance abuse, and many others.

I did not see emphasis on White and Asian people that are hungry, poor, involved in crime, etc. I see Latino, Mexicans, and Black people instead. Meaning, to generalize the many incidents about Colored and White races is that it is always the White race's fault whatever happened to the Colored people. My theory as a Doctor Of Philosophy is that in order for the society to know that there is no favoritism to any race, such as White and Colored people, therefore, even if the Colored People are at fault, the White race has to be blamed. That's why in this book of mine, I titled it "Skin Color Does Not Matter, What Matters Is What's in the Mind and Heart" of each one of us.

Solutions to issues of discrimination should be through judgments based on the reality of the incidents, and not based on skin color. For example, Black Lives Matter, and why are Colored people offended if it says, All Lives Matter? Which truly means all lives matter, including Asians, White, Black, Mexicans, etc.

If the system categorizes individuals through skin color and by race, the purpose of record-keeping of a person becomes too complicated. For record-keeping, it must be through Citizenship as an AMERICAN CITIZEN, or a person could be NOT an American Citizen. Therefore, the investigation fully fulfills its purpose. To categorize an individual through skin color, there are always prejudices. Why don't we start looking onto our citizenships instead of skin color? When people live in America and are documented, they become American citizens, whether their skin color is black, white, red, yellow, brown, tan, etc. They are Americans, no matter what. Therefore, the problem of this country should divide people not by color but by citizenship. Are these Americans legitimately Americans? That's it. It is that simple!

But, Hey! What's in Your Mind & Heart Matters

Why can't Congress put this together? Okay, I understand, there are many illegal aliens in this country. Fine, then look for those and process and sort their situation and those eligible to become American citizens could process their papers to become Americans and take advantage of their tax dollars. They must pay taxes just like Americans. Those others that cannot stay in America due to rules and regulations and in any other situations that make them truly illegal should be deported to their own country. Also, why is it easy for illegal people to come to America? My experience coming to America in 1984 cost money and time to process to come to America in those years, the 1980s. I waited for years to become an American Citizen. I came to America as a worker of a Chinese company, Lucky Company. I became an American Citizen in the year 1990.

Then some people think I came from the border between Mexico and America. My experiences as an American Citizen since 1984-1990 and was a Filipino Citizen from 1957 to 1984 were very shocking. On June 28, 2012, again another man at Walmart thinks that I am a mail-order bride or a Filipina that got married to a soldier in the Philippines and came to America. He was so serious about it, telling me to always take care of my husband because without my husband, I would not be here in America. What a shameful comment about this issue. My husband was not a soldier, and I did not meet my husband in the Philippines. I met my husband in the United States of America. I did not meet my husband as a soldier, and I was not a mail-order bride. Besides, I do not even understand what a "MAIL-ORDER BRIDE" is. What an IGNORANT person that was who I met at Walmart telling and guessing that I am a mail bride. To clarify, NOT all Filipinas meet a white man in the Philippines, and not all Filipinas are mail-order brides, whatever that is. Do not generalize all situations here on earth of plenty. Because EVERYONE has different situations and personality, lifestyles, practices, and living situations, and different growing up.

Do not generalize that all Filipinos have the same life situations. Use quantity and measure using analysis through numbers and give a percentage of your analysis. That's how you categorize something that counts in percentages. If you do not understand what I am saying, just to tell you DO NOT GENERALIZE situations, culture, and or population in that category.

The stereotype of Filipina women is an ongoing practice by Canadians, British Columbians, and the United States according to sources. Filipinos' experiences from the past in World War II such that they were called savages, childlike, and unmotivated are still in the minds of many traditionalists. Due to unknown names of Filipina women traditionalists or society may call them Asian Americans, Pacific Islanders, Asians, Orientals, Mexicans, Spanish, Puerto Ricans, and Hawaiians. In this book, a brief clarification of Filipino descent will be explored based on literature reviews.

But, Hey! What's in Your Mind & Heart Matters

However, the focus of this book, *"Hey! What Matter Is In the Minds and Hearts"* not by skin color such as the stereotype affecting Filipina women who are documented workers around the world. Because of these stereotypes of Filipina women working overseas, Filipino-Americans, and other individuals of Asian descent are affected due to society's ignorance of cultural identity. For example, in my experience as a Filipina descent who has been in the United States for more than 40 years, some people still consider me an alien or Mexican, assuming that I am an illegal alien in this country.

During my college years, I utilized NVivo 9 to extract statistics and methods for comparing Asian American and Pacific Islander (AAPI) experiences, along with an exploration of the history of Spanish and American colonialism in the Philippines to clarify some issues related to the stereotypes. Additionally, I drew insights from Bryan Sykes' book titled "The Seven Daughters of Eve," which explores the dispersion of our ancestors before the existence of humanity. Sykes' book delves into the question of where we genetically originated and emphasizes the importance of education on various cultures to combat ignorance.

Sykes, a scientist, underscores the significance of our genetic material, which carries a message from our ancestors in every cell of our body, handed down from generation to generation (Sykes, 2001, pg. 2). While history education is crucial, it has unfortunately been removed from the classroom. Sykes asserts that the information about who we are as humans never fades and that modern technology helps decipher messages from the past through DNA and genetics.

Sykes' genetic ancestry research reveals the migration patterns of Homo sapiens, and he discusses the discovery of the Iceman's body in the Alps. This naked body, found at a high altitude in the Alps, was initially thought to be a modern mountaineer. However, further investigation revealed the icepick near the body to be thousands of years old. The Iceman's remains, now frozen in the Institute of Forensic in Innsbruck, Austria, provided crucial information about our shared ancestry (Sykes, 2001, page 4).

According to Sykes, the Iceman lived 5,000 to 5,350 years ago and was determined to be European through DNA analysis. In his book, "The Seven Daughters of Eve," Sykes explores the genetic lineages of individuals, giving names such as Ursula, Xenia, Helena, Velda, and Tara. While this book will only mention a few names, the broader point is to understand that as humans, we share a common ancestry, emphasizing that skin color does not matter; what matters is what's in our hearts and minds.

*"From the remains in Cheddar Gorge we had extracted direct proof of the genetic continuity between people living today and the hunters of the Upper Paleolithic. We now knew that this*

*unbroken thread, accurately and faithfully recorded in our DNA, stretched back beyond the beginnings of history, beyond the ages of iron, bronze and copper to an ancient world of ice, forest and tundra. Only the exceedingly slow beat of the molecular clock separated the DNA we found in Cheddar Man from the DNA in our two utterly modern descendants Adrian Targett and Cuthbert the butler. The evolutionary reconstruction we had done on the DNA from thousands of living Europeans had pointed us to that conclusion, and eventually we had found physical evidence to validate it. Now we also had the crucial endorsement from another genetic system altogether, the Y-chromosome, of the assertion that our genetic roots do indeed go back deep into the Paleolithic"* (Sykes, 2001, page 195).

Based on the scientific study, the given name Tara belonged to a woman who lived in northern Italy approximately 17,000 years ago. Tara's descendants migrated along the coast into France, joining a large group of hunters tracking game across the tundra of northern Europe. Eventually, Tara's lineage crossed the dry land that would later become the English Channel, moving across Ireland. The clan named after Tara traces its origins to this ancient Celtic kingdom (Sykes, 2001, Pages 8-13).

As for Ursula, she was the second child of her mother and was born during a period much colder than the weather we experience today. In the Great Ice Age according to Sykes (2001)

*"Ursula was born in a shallow cave cut into the cliffs at the foot of what is now Mount Parnassus, close to what was to become the ancient Greek classical site of Delphi. The cave mouth looked out across a wide plain a thought foot below which led away to the sea twenty miles off to the south"* (page 202).

Ursula's clan had an unbroken lineage, similar to the first modern humans who successfully colonized various parts of Europe. Direct descendants of Neanderthals, particularly in Britain and Scandinavia, constitute about "11 percent of modern Europeans who are direct maternal descendants of Ursula" (Sykes, 2001, Pages 208-212). Her ancestors migrated from the Near East through Turkey, crossed the Bosphorus with freshwater to the north, and settled around the Black Sea.

After Ursula's death, about 20,000 years passed, bringing us closer to the present, when the world was experiencing colder conditions than ever before, around 25,000 years ago. During this period, the Neanderthals had disappeared, and modern humans in Europe took over, settling in regions such as the Great Plains, Britain, and the west of Casa Kazakhstan in the east. The temperatures were harsh, ranging from 20 to zero degrees for many weeks, creating inhospitable conditions. However, the situation was also beneficial at time due to *"Europe tundra was also teeming with life and good things to eat massive herds of bison and reindeer rather move slowly over the plains feeding on the rich growth of grass and Moses smaller herds of wild horse and wild were also there to be hunted but that dominant animal with no enemies to fear was the gigantic woolly mammoth no natural enemies that is until the humans arrive*" Xenia was born in this era (Sykes, 2001).

I am providing a brief explanation about where we came from as humans. It could be more than that, such as why our skin color differs in different countries. Skin color can change depending on where the sun settles and shines. This is one of the many reasons why skin color changes NATURALLY for every human who lives in a place where the weather or atmosphere differs, such as snow, heat, cold, and of course, the DNA of a person and their parents' origins.

# CHAPTER 6

# Examples of Women Stories Across Cultures

We as women are shaped differently than men. As you know, women were trained to be feminine, as our body shape is different than that of men. Therefore, women act differently than men. Historical ignorance affects the past and the present times. In most schools today, historical lectures are removed, and therefore, the ignorance of our young and old minds is empty of historical knowledge from the past that affects us all as humans. Let me give you an example of where women came from and how women existed in this world. For example, the study of women in this book is explained in this section—their experiences and what and how they were going through may not be the source of balancing between the situations of women but a fraction of how women go through many hardships in life in the previous era and at the present times.

Let us explore briefly and compare women in the prehistoric era to those in the ancient Near East. Although scientists found some evidence of women depicted in visual art in the prehistoric era, there were no definite depictions of humans, either men or women, who created these specific arts, images, or objects. Scientists could only speculate by analyzing artifacts and images found. Artists in the

Paleolithic era depicted women in visual arts as nude, with big breasts, flabby, wide thighs and hips, and an indistinct face. Why? According to Slatkin, this was to represent that fertility in womanhood was more important than the perfect figure. Since writing was not invented in this era, these images serve as narratives, lectures, and teaching tools within the group. For example, Venus in Willendorf in the year 30,000 to 00 BC, made in limestone, is one of sixty statuettes found from caves from Southern France to Eastern Russia. This statuette's belly is round, with visual emphasis on the pubic area and thighs. It is not important to see the face of this woman's image. It seems that in the Paleolithic era, artists were not concerned with faces and the perfection of figures.

Women in the Paleolithic era concerned with womanhood and how important it was to be a woman and be pregnant and have children. They passed on what they believed to their children through images and illustrations. We can only speculate that perhaps women were artists, farmers, and crafts makers. Women must have created their images because, in the Paleolithic era, men were hunters, and obviously, women were left in the cave, and they must have had time to draw and care for their children!

According to Slatkin, Near Eastern women were very rarely portrayed as nude images. Women were depicted creating textiles, and craftworks, for example, weaving, harvesting, and caring for animals and children. Evidence found indicates that women were also employed in the temples and palaces. Women were also portrayed as priestesses. For example, the Calcite Disk of Enheduanna, Daughter of Sargon the Great, depicts one function of a woman as a priestess. Although Enheduanna is a priestess, her figure is depicted standing behind the man while the man performs the ritual.

Furthermore, when political power took over and became centralized, women were not allowed to make decisions. Women became dependent on men. Women were also the private property of men, including their children. Parents arranged their daughters' marriages. For the daughters of the poor, slavery was the only option for financial reasons. If couples had many children, they (especially the husband) had economic worth in society. A woman with many children had advantages regarding her status.

In addition, there was no abortion in this era due to abortion being a serious crime. So, the occupation of women became more focused on bearing and educating children, household tasks like weaving, needlework, and music-making. However, according to Slatkin, women were not totally excluded in regard to status. Women were given equal rights to men in some legal and financial transactions. Slave women also participated in contributing to economic development. Women held jobs like scribes, midwives, singers, town keepers, and chemists. Females who were highly skilled in weaving were valuable in this era and in great demand from the upper classes.

In conclusion, it seems that women worked for survival purposes. They did not have the right to make decisions on their own. They had to work for financial reasons, were sold for financial reasons, and married for financial reasons. It was always for the sake of society and for the husband's benefit. Regarding what a woman wanted in her life, it seemed they did not have the right to choose.

Let us compare Hatshepsut and Nefertiti in limitation and power. Nefertiti and Hatshepsut differed in the way they were portrayed. Nefertiti was portrayed in a feminist manner with an emphasis on beauty, while Hatshepsut was portrayed as a man, with an emphasis on power and strength as a man. Hatshepsut was the principal wife of her half-brother Thutmose II, who also had a minor wife and a son from that minor wife, named Thutmose III.

In Hatshepsut's later reign, she was portrayed as a man. So, she had many guises. Her insignia as the king's principal wife. She wanted to be called "God's Wife"; images were flat-chested and had a body shaped like a man. On the other hand, she had also been shaped like a woman earlier in her reign. When the time came for Thutmose III to reign, Hatshepsut was still in joint kingship with their husband, Thutmose II. She stepped down as queen and fully adopted the title of king.

In addition, Hatshepsut had a daughter named Nefura and

was referred to as God's Wife. Hatshepsut's chancellor, named Senmut, also took care of Nefura but was fired after Hatshepsut found out that Senmut was too influential and powerful. So, Hatshepsut was the female who played so many roles in her lifetime. Furthermore, Hatshepsut supervised the construction of a temple and performed jobs that only a king was able to perform, such as ordering a pair of obelisks for the temple—an indication of a powerful king's responsibilities. Obelisks were offered to the gods in an impressive mortuary temple.

The achievements of Hatshepsut were illustrated in relief and served as a design for her funerary cult's rituals, for example, the Funerary Temple of Queen Hatshepsut in Dier El-Bahri. She also performed tasks like trading valuable goods. This temple has the largest stone architectural monument built by Hatshepsut. Evidence found that she was portrayed as a king in Egypt in her time. So, what's the difference between Hatshepsut and Nefertiti? When there is a change in society, artists seem to follow the change and create images to record the people and their activities.

Unlike Hatshepsut, Nefertiti was portrayed as a woman of beauty, with an aspect of motherhood and gracefulness. The perfection of her figure is more emphasized in the details. She was also portrayed as a king according to evidence found, but based on my reading, she was portrayed more as beautiful, motherly, and a queen with overall femininity as a woman. Nefertiti was the principal wife of Akhenaton, previously called Amenhotep IV. In this era, Akhenaton gave up worshipping the Polytheistic gods and goddesses of Egypt. He created a new religion based on his own god, the only universal god, Aton, the sun disk. Artists portrayed Akhenaton's figure as both a man and a woman figure. The figure looked like a human being with a protruding belly, thick lips, big eyes, but an unknown image of that time.

However, with Akhenaton's queen Nefertiti, the figure was different. Nefertiti was portrayed as delicate and graceful with a sensitive manner and a curving contour. Although the bust was not finished, the artist was very specific in illustrating this beautiful woman named Nefertiti, which means "The beautiful one is here." There were many queens, but no other queen images were shown in the tombs, mortuary temple, and sanctuary.

Nefertiti was very important to Aton's religious time. Her appearance in the temple of Karnak offering to god was similar to Aten's importance of Hatshepsut's offering jar to the gods. This task was supposed to be for the king, but these two women performed tasks that were intended for a king, for example, Stele, Altar at Amarna, Nefertiti, and Akhenaten symbolized the new god. In this, Nefertiti was the Virgin Mary image. She was portrayed as a queen, and later evidence found that she was also depicted wearing a crown like that of a king.

Today's previous generation and to these days, human manipulation, such as changing women and men's bodies to fulfill their thoughts of what they think is needed at that time, and to these days, such as the society needs men. On the other hand, women were unable to do what men were supposed to be in society as a woman. In similarity, these days and at this moment of humanity, such as impersonating sex, such as a woman to become a man and a man to become a woman, is such a confusing world then, and now is so visible.

Such as what I witnessed when I travel internationally, I am confused *When a man mentions the name of his wife, which is a man's name, and a woman would say her wife's name is a woman's name, it is a very confusing world. I do not know anymore what to call when a man is a woman, and shall I say ma'am or sir. Conversely, when a woman says she is a husband of a woman, shall I call her Sir or Ma'am?* Such a very confusing world! I am so confused. The world is changing through individuals' imagination of who they are and what they want to be. It is very unimaginable and unrealistic. Faking yourself can be a very disturbing kind of life in the temporary walk on earth. It seems out of line because a man is a man, and a woman is supposed to be a woman. What I believe is that God made a woman and a man. Twisting that around, I do believe that is against God's creation. Because He created a MAN and a WOMAN only. What do you think? When a boy is born, he is a man when he grows up, and he is a HE. When a girl is born, she is a woman when SHE grows up. The "SHE" is a woman, and the "HE" is a man. When a human being reverses the gender of an individual, such as a man is a woman, and a woman is a man, that is very confusing! Therefore, humans who change their gender from a man to a woman or a woman to a man, I am very sure that these individuals are against God's creation. It's the person's choice changing his or her gender from what God had created for these individuals. The manipulation of GENDER is not God's given identity for these individuals. That's my spiritual theory of this type of lifestyle. So, I questioned myself, and I was very confused. I then did research about it.

A long time ago, society needed mothers to bear a baby boy; therefore, if the baby were a girl, parents would use a doctor to alter the private part of a newborn little girl into male private, a boy. Today, a test tube baby or shall we call it a baby that will be preserved in a tube that can alter the sexual organ of the baby at parents' request. This practice was hidden. Today, it is now visible, and society is trying to make this human practice and lifestyle become normal and to others, it is very confusing. I did research about the consequences for these types of practices and lifestyles. Therefore, is a trans disease ongoing in this generation? The XYY is a disease syndrome called Androgen Insensitivity Syndrome.

The difference between the two women was on Nefertiti; she

was able to perform limitedly as a king and still retain her femininity. However, Hatshepsut, who took on many more male responsibilities, could not retain her femininity but was powerful as a king. Nefertiti never was a king or had power on her own, only through her husband (Google, 2023).

Let us compare women in Egypt to those in Greece. There was evidence found in which one of the temples that women in Egypt were portrayed in funerary monuments and in tombs. The illustrations of women were as slender images, never married, or maybe never having borne a child. Skin color distinguished men and women in this era, and women were portrayed with lighter skin than men. The artist visualized the light-colored skin as women in upper-class status because women usually stayed indoors. In this era, women worked inside the home.

Furthermore, the king's mother and king's principal wife played important roles in the ritual. Also, kingship and queenship performances were considered divine. The position of a king and queen was of equal importance in some instances in this population; for example, the Pair Statue of Menkaure and His Queen, from Giza, in Dynasty IV, year 2559-1571 B.C. Menkaure, the king, and Khamerernebty II, the queen, stand together at almost the same height, which is a sign of the equality of this man and woman.

In the fifth century B.C. in Athens, Greece, there was evidence of men and women's status of separation. Men were busy in public affairs, while women stayed home to do their responsibilities. Women were limited to going anywhere except to the graveyard and to fetch water. Meanwhile, men had an opportunity to learn art and were able to explore and educate themselves. While women were taught how to make crafts, embroideries, take care of children, and do household tasks, they were not allowed to get an education.

However, women were provided dowry rights, but they had no legal rights. They were not eligible to sign documents or manage businesses. Also, female infanticide was practiced by Greeks in 1100 circa 560 B.C., women were depicted in 800 B.C., and it contained from the fourth to the first century B.C. For all classes of women, their job was to weave textiles and embroidery. Therefore, I have added here just a few examples about women of today (Google, 2023). Today's young generation is going back to the past and making up themselves as who they want to be but only to ruin themselves such as trans disease, XYY and/or XXX is a disease syndrome, called Androgen Insensitivity Syndrome.

# CHAPTER 7

# Women, Art, & Society

Women in previous eras faced many issues of immorality. Therefore, the next generation must focus on implementing morality. There are still lingering beliefs from past eras, such as the avoidance of inter-cultural marriages, like Asian and White, White, and Black, due to various cultural beliefs.

### Artemisia's Life Story:

Artemisia Gentileschi was born in Rome on July 8, 1593. Her father, Orazio Gentileschi, trained her in painting. She was the oldest among four siblings. R. Ward Bissell, in his latest book titled "Artemisia Gentileschi and the Authority of Art," mentioned that Artemisia had five children, contrasting with Garrard's earlier information that she only had two children listed in the registrar. After Garrard's writing, Bissell found that two of Artemisia's children used different last names, and possibly one child was with her husband, Stiattesi, during their stay in Florence (Bissell, 158).

Artemisia's earliest painting, "Susanna and The Elders," was created in 1610-1612 and is now housed at Pommersfelden. This painting coincided with her torture in the municipal court. According to Bissell, "Tassie and the glare of public scrutiny will then complete this examination of Gentileschi's extraordinary beginnings…Susanna and The Elders…the elders hatching their plot, vaulting upon the defenseless woman, demanding that she submit sexually on pain of public denunciation on a trumped-up charge of adultery with a young man, cautioning silence; Susanna startled, feeling violated, confronted with a moral decision, and resisted" (Bissell, 2). Perhaps Artemisia's feelings were similar to Susanna's. She had been violated and confronted morally, and resistance was not an option. Young Artemisia, at 17 years of age, was frightened when a conniving older man, Tassi, mentally, physically, and emotionally raped her. According to Bissell, her future was a "representation of highly human distress," and "…some commentators have found in the Susanna manifestations of Artemisia's personal situation. There are undeniable parallels between the tone and conduct of Agostino Tassi 1612 and Susanna narrative" (Bissell, 7-8).

Artemisia went to Venice and painted "Esther Before Ahasuerus" in 1620. This painting was mistakenly dated 1640 by the Museum and was the date of the revision in Rome. Artemisia worked in Rome, but she was not hired, although she had sold her works in earlier years. In 1630, she went to Naples and brought her style called Caravaggism. This was a revolutionary technique of tenebrism, a dramatic, selective illumination of form out of deep shadow that became one of the hallmarks of Baroque painting. Artemisia learned to be an independent artist and excelled in the art world. According to Garrard, there was not a lot of writing about Artemisia, although in her era, she was doing very well as a female artist. Perhaps Artemisia was trapped as a female artist in a male-dominant society.

Since females were not eligible for a formal path to artistic careers, such as training with more than an established master, travel, or memberships in a guild, Artemisia's apprenticeships to her father would have been her only access to the profession (Garrard 16-17). It was hard to trace Artemisia's training experience because she was trained in an informal setting at home, with her father. Garrard continued that Artemisia could not write and could only read a little. On the other hand, the book titled "Artemisia Gentileschi and The Authority Art" by R. Ward Bissell included lots of letters Artemisia created and read, but there was no evidence if they were written by her. Her earliest paintings seemed to reflect intensive training. Although Artemisia couldn't write and read, she developed much training in the language of art. Why did Artemisia seem unpopular in her era? Is it because she concentrated on female bodies, not male nudes like male artists popular at this time? We also wonder what Artemisia's motive and message were in her paintings.

In this era, the theme included nude males and Biblical figures. For example, Orazio Gentileschi painted _St. Francis Supported by An Angel_ in 1600-1603. Caravaggio painted "Ecstasy of St. Francis" in 1595. Caravaggio painted nude male figures in 1509-1511, and Orazio Gentileschi and Agostino Tassi printed "Musical Concert" in 1611-12. However, Artemisia's themes mostly revolved around women, for example, "Cleopatra," "The Rape of Lucretia," "Esther Before Ahasuerus," and "Judith Slaying Holofernes." These illustrations depicted brave and powerful women allegorically overpowering the masculinity of men.

For example, one scholar commented that "Judith Slaying Head of Holofernes" is a connotation of either revenge or an expression of anger, hurt, or power. The only way Artemisia could express her feelings was through the language of art, which was much more powerful than words. Artemisia's art seems to speak for itself, conveying women's struggles in the hands of a patriarchal society. Her unselfish portrayal includes other women of her era, raising questions about Artemisia's struggles in the hands of a patriarchal society.

Furthermore, during a visit to the Metropolitan Museum of Art, Artemisia Gentileschi's "Esther Before Ahasuerus" painting was displayed. According to Mann Christiansen, Vashti, a queen of King Ahasuerus, was summoned but refused to appear at a feast and dance in front of two king's guests. Vashti was disavowed and replaced with Esther, who fasted for three days with her people, the Jews. Esther, weak when appearing in front of King Ahasuerus, fainted but managed to stand with the help of a slave, breaking court etiquette and risking her death. The King, instead, touched her with his scepter to indicate her special status (Mann 373). This painting was among Artemisia's most ambitious illustrations of women, recounting the story of a Jewish heroine.

According to the museum information, this painting was a gift of Eleanor Dorone Ingesol in 1969, with a size of 10 feet by 9 feet. It was displayed with another big painting, probably 14 feet by 12 feet, that is not Artemisia's. Some chips were noticeable on the frame of Artemisia's painting, and the canvas appeared to be slightly broken. It didn't look like a canvas but more like wood. The brass or gold tone had faded a bit on the frame. Across from "Esther Before Ahasuerus," Caravaggio's painting "The Holy Family," painted in the year 1571-1610, was displayed along with "The Denial of St. Peter," painted at the same time. Other artists' works were also displayed, such as "The Parable of The Mote and the Bean" by Dominico Fetti in the year 1588-1623, and "Paradise" by Calo Saraceni in the year 1579-1620.

Many scholars debated Artemisia's works, especially "Esther Before Ahasuerus." According to Bissell, the setup of Artemisia's canvas was derived from one of Paolo Veronese's conceptions, which Gentileschi could have seen in Venice. Other aspects led directly to pictures created for Florence after Gentileschi's first appearances there (Bissell 74). Bissell continued that Rutilio Manetti's "Rogher and Alcina," dated 1622-23, and

"Massinnisa and Sophanisba," dated 1625, were somewhat connected with Artemisia's "Esther Before Ahasuerus" regarding male and female encounters. Scholars agree that Artemisia created "Esther Before Ahasuerus" in Venice in 1620 and revised her work when she went back to Rome in 1640. According to Garrard, this revision was clearly seen in an x-ray. Artemisia covered the dog and the dwarf near Ahasuerus to fit in with the Roman theme and style (Garrard 72).

The scene of Esther was melodramatic in flavor. Esther was illustrated in a foreshortened position where she did not fall totally, but only leaned her head onto a slave. This leveled her with King Ahasuerus. Bissell intelligently observed and analyzed Esther, and he continued that Gentileschi's textures and source must be recognized in a reading of "Esther Before Ahasuerus." It was from the "Apocryphal Book of Esther" where in Ahasuerus raised from his throne in mildness of Spirit, not the Biblical account which has the King extending his golden scepter, an act, and a symbol of male authority that Artemisia avoids (Bissell 75). Artemisia Gentileschi wished to make some statement about female dominance. Garrard mentioned that Artemisia's "majestic demeanor and extraordinary pictorial status given to Esther" connected with her. In the 1620s, not the 1640s, was the strongest period of heroic female imagery for Artemisia. The juxtaposition of the king and queen in the painting was balanced carefully, conveying Esther's womanly ability to influence the king's "judgment through persuasion rather than overt defiance" (Garrard 72). To Artemisia, it should be a traditional and an *appropriate male-female relationship.*

In conclusion, regarding the unique illustration style of Artemisia, I agree that she was a master of her craft and an illustrator of the thoughts and feelings within each of her characters. Artemisia managed to capture and illustrate what was in her mind and heart, connecting these emotions to her subjects, making her work truly unique. Furthermore, Artemisia's art resonated with viewers, including myself as a writer and researcher of Artemisia. Today, both women and men can pursue the arts, exercising their talents to create unique and meaningful artworks. "The woman who walks alone is likely to find herself in places no one has ever been before." (Albert Einstein, Theoretical Physicist 1879-1955).

## The Etruscans Women:

According to the video I watched, the Etruscans had an advanced civilization in an ancient world where, at the time, Roman dwellings and settlements were made from clusters of straw and mud, forming huts. The Etruscans ruled a peninsula starting from the north of the Arno River south of the Tiber River in Italy. Their artistic talents and culture originated from Minor Asia and the Near East.

If we go back to the Near East, according to Slatkin, women

in this era worked in the temples and palaces. The lives of women averaged 25 to 35 years, and they were expected to be married and have children. The more children they had, the more valuable they were in the community. Parents arranged their daughters' marriages. Although some women were not totally excluded, evidence shows that they handled businesses, could sign legal documents, and held a higher status. Female slaves also participated in economic development.

In Asia Minor, now Turkey, in Anatolia, according to Kleiner, excavations at Thacila of Catal Huyuk and elsewhere have shown that the Central Anatolian plateau was the site of a flourishing Neolithic culture between 7000 and 5000 B.C. Twelve successive building levels excavated at Catal Huyuk between 1961 and 1965 have been dated between 6500 and 5700 B.C. (Kleiner, page 13). This is where we can trace the life of Neolithic-era Asia Minor women. During this period, they created wall paintings, plaster reliefs, animal heads, and bucrania (bovine skull). The symbol of masculinity was a bull's horn, while in a separate room, the symbol of fertility was a plaster breasts projected from the walls. Excavators also found statuettes of female figures, eight to twelve inches long.

In summary, by examining these two cultures, we can gain insights into Etruscan women and their culture. According to website writings I pulled out, the status of women in the Etruscan era was of different from that of Greeks and Romans "...*Greeks were basically misogynists, and the Romans were chauvinistic, but the Etruscan rather treated their women well.*" (http//www/geocities.com 3/01/04). According to Random House Webster Dictionary misogynist means, *"woman hater or hatred or hostility toward women, and chauvinistic means, zealous and aggressive patriotism or blind enthusiasm for military glory, biased devotion to any group, attitude or cause.*" (Random House Webster Dictionary).

A journal by Richard De Puma delves into mirrors that Etruscan women treasured the most. Almost 3,500 mirrors were discovered in a cemetery excavation. According to De Puma, the mirror designs were elaborate, featuring various images depicting everyday life and mythology of the Etruscan civilization. A mirror was such a special gift to women that they buried it with a woman when she died. It symbolized their status, holding both funerary and religious connotations. The mirror consisted of designs depicting four large nude female figures with wings, an Etruscan deity or nymph named Lasa. A severed head represented Orpheus. The interpretation of this excellent engraving suggests that Orpheus is prophesying a happy and fruitful marriage for a mythical couple, who, in a sense, are the archetype of an Etruscan couple about to be married—an appealing hypothesis given that mirrors were often given as wedding gifts to Etruscan women (De Puma, 2).

Furthermore, as a Macedonian king, Orpheus was skilled in

music using a lyre. Unfortunately, Orpheus did not allow women into his religion, so women cut him into pieces and threw them into the sea. Anyone who overpowered women made them angry, and so they got together to defeat men. Women in this era were very powerful, but it only applied to aristocratic women.

In addition, the image on the handle of this mirror is a female figure with wings, pulling a long piece of drapery over her left shoulder. She wears elaborate earrings, a necklace, and a diadem. The severed head of Orpheus lies on the ground and is surrounded by four large figures, plus Lasa and a standing female. De Puma wasn't sure if the four figures were women because the handle was broken. On the right of the handle is a seated man with a tablet in his hand and a stylus in his mouth. He is flanked by one nude female and two nude males who look at the seated scribe. The male is in the center, with a spear and wears drapery tied around his neck. Another male figure appears with a ribbon and a flower in his hand.

Larissa Bonfante, one of the authors, *The Classical Etruscan Women* discusses an Etruscan couple who went to Rome. *"As the man and his highborn wife looked down on the city that was to be their new home, an eagle came down and plucked off the husband's hat and flew back into the sky above the covered wagon, then swooping back down to put the hat back on the man's head, the eagle disappeared into the heavens." (Bonfante 243).* The man's wife was unknowledgeable about interpreting omens, and they were sure that these ambitions would lead to a joyful journey to Rome. The wife's name is Tanaquil, and she is an Etruscan queen of King Lucius Tarquin. She earlier killed her father and father-in-law, ran over her father's body with a carriage, and stained herself with her father's blood. Tarquin the proud King was frightened by this incident. Additionally, a Roman matron, Lucretia, was raped by his son.

Etruscan and Roman women were totally opposite in terms of culture, behaviors, and responsibilities. According to Bonfante, Etruscan princesses attended luxurious dinner parties with other people of the same status. Once a Greek historian named, Theopompus wrote: *"Etruscans, who were extraordinarily pleasure loving... that the slave girls wait on the man naked... it is normal for Etruscans to share their women in common. These women take great care of their bodies and exercise bare, exposing their bodies even before men and among themselves; for it is not shameful for them to appear almost naked. They dine not with their husbands, but with any man who happens to be present; and they toast anyone they want to"* (Bonfanti, 248).

In addition, Bonfante continued, stating that men made love with every woman, and Etruscan women had children without knowing the father of each child. The culture and behavior were imitated by these children who did the same as they had learned and been brought up. Sex was accustomed and considered a normal activity for Etruscans, not shameful. However, when asked,

Bonfante was not certain how much of this account was true (Bonfante, 249). Therefore, today sexual activity is a practice of many women in this generation and the previous generation.

Immorality still exists to this day. However, I, myself, always follow what my parents say, "no sex before marriage." When the message ingrained in your mind is that "No Sex Before Marriage," it protects you from many sexual temptations. So, what matters is what's in our mind and heart that we have developed since we were young.

Bonfante continues with the story of Lucretia. She was busy doing her responsibility, directing women weaving wool. King Tarquin's son was drunk and raped Lucretia. Not only did he threaten her, but he also violated the law of hospitality. According to Bonfante, this was the beginning of why Etruscans were driven from Rome, and when the Roman republic was established.

In summary, images carved on mirrors, wall paintings, and artifacts are evidence of how different the Etruscans and Roman women were. According to writing on the web, women were treated well in the Etruscans' era, while, according to Bonfante, a Greek historian named Theopompus, wrote that nudity, lusty living, and sex were ordinary attractions. In De Puma's writing, Etruscan women were special to the community.

So, according to the website writing I pulled, Greeks were

misogynists, and the Romans were chauvinistic. We may ask, did this really happen? How did Theopompus, the Greek historian, get this idea if it didn't happen in reality? How about the ancient civilization in Asia Minor and the near east? According to Slatkin, parents arranged their daughter's marriage, and women had good standing if they had many children, and men had many concubines. Is this one of the reasons for what Etruscan culture became? Again, Etruscans saw sex and nudity as normal, contrasting with Asia Minor, which is now Turkey and Anatolia. Is this why today Turkish and Anatolian women are covered with veils to avoid attraction to the opposite sex?

Therefore, we now have rules to follow such rules *"no sex before marriage"* since when I was growing up and my parent's belief of "no sex before marriage" rules since in the 1900. We hope to continue until these days and in the future for our children and grandchildren's well-being. Make marriage a sacred event for a longer unity of husband and wife, giving our children a good influence regarding the unity of a man and a woman. According to Einstein, "The world is a dangerous place to live, not because of the people who are evil, but because of the people who don't do anything about it." (Albert Einstein, Theoretical Physicist 1879-1955).

### Carolina Maria De Jesus' Life Story:

The life story of women struggling with hunger and famine, such as the story I would like to tell in this chapter of Carolina Maria De Jesus. Her story is an example of women without a husband taking care of their children by themselves. Hearing and knowing about women struggling, perhaps, makes you dizzy, and sometimes you faint and lose consciousness. Your mind is confused, and you fight for energy. You press your stomach tightly so you will feel a little relief from the pain of hunger, and you say words from your mouth unconsciously, *"This will pass away."*

For those who have experienced this type of hunger feeling in life, yes, "This will pass away." For those human beings, especially children who live in hunger and poverty, and constantly struggle to survive is all we can say to them… *"I have sympathy."* These people don't need sympathy! They need empathy! This is the feeling of hunger and famine! Feel these people! I may say.

A woman, Carolina Maria de Jesus, is living by scavenging in the trash of the city's streets. She was born in 1915 in Sacramento, the southern part of the Minas Gerais border of Sao Paulo State in Brazil. Carolina has three children living in a shack. The shack is made of boards, tins, and junk put together into a shelter. The struggle of looking for food every mealtime and looking for water to drink is an everyday event in this favela. A favela is a place where poor people live. Carolina describes this place: *"The governor's place is the living room. The mayor's office is the dining room, and the city is the garden. And the favela is the backyard where they throw the garbage."* (Moffat 293).

According to St. Clair's manuscript, "They had thrown a lot of sausage in the garbage. I sorted them out once they were rotten. I don't want to grow weak, and I can't afford to buy." (St. Clair, 85). She also mentioned in her diary about the boy in the favela who was looking for lunch in the garbage and found rotten meat! The boy said he was very hungry. He had not eaten for many days, and it is better to eat rotten meat than to feel hunger. The boy ate it, and after six hours, the boy's body blew up, and his toes and fingers were so big, his whole body looked like a tightly blown balloon. Carolina de Jesus witnesses and experiences this horrible environment.

Every single day, she looks for water and food to eat. Her goal is to feed her three children. Her body aches after a day of carrying paper to sell for money to buy food. Then, she rests and thinks about where to look for paper to sell the next day. Sometimes if she can't find paper, she looks for bottles to trade for bread for food that day. Every day, she goes to the garbage and looks for cans, bottles, and paper to sell.

One day, she sells cans for only 13 cruzeiros, which is not enough to buy bread. She is so frightened of not being able to feed her children and having them go to sleep hungry. In her diary (made of foraged scraps of paper she sewed into notebooks), she describes what's going on in the favela. She wants to tell everyone of the suffering and the others in the favela, including politicians and the entire country of Brazil.

Book written by Ruth Sidel titled, *"In women and children last: The Plight of Poor Women in Affluent America."* Ruth Sidel mentioned: "When we think of poverty in poor countries, we think of emaciated or swollen-bellied children starving to death… people dying side by side… large families huddling together in squatters' settlements that exist in most Latin American cities, children begging outside…"(Sidel 5). Here in America, the image of poverty means standing in line for food in soup kitchen, staying temporarily in welfare hotels, a homeless woman sleeping in the doorway with her belongings, and families with no heat in winter.

In *Tyranny of Kindness, Dismantling the System to End Poverty in America"* Theresa Funiciello says: *"Here too the problem has been I'm frustrated, yet it's relatively simple there is too little habitable housing for all who need it at rents poor people can pay, the burning question is not a shortage of dollars but their allocation. The constant is politics."* (Funinciello 162).

The struggle of Carolina Maria De Jesus, as one of the women in poverty in Brazil, is similar to women who face poverty in America. The difference is that women in America are not allowed to pick up rotten sausage out of the garbage. There are no tins, bottles, or scrap paper to be picked up for sale. Shacks cannot be built without meeting government requirements and zoning laws.

Additionally, Carolina Maria De Jesus, being a black woman, uneducated, and a single mother, is more likely to face discrimination than other women in poverty. She consistently maintains a balance in defining who she is, preserving her dignity, and teaching her children respect for others.

Furthermore, Carolina Maria De Jesus was never married to a man and avoids having men in her life. The reasons why women, in general, avoid men in their lives and whether this contributes to the prevalence of women and children in poverty are questions worth exploring. An example is given of a man named Anselmo in the favela where Carolina lives, who brought a pregnant woman to be his companion. *"When the woman gave birth to a boy, he started to mistreat her, he beat her and throw her out of the house."* (St. Clair, 97). De Jesus had three men in her life but was never married to any of them. One was from where she was employed as a maid, and when she got pregnant, her employer threw her out. Then, the second one was a social worker, a white man who fathered her children and occasionally gave her money. Although there were men interested in her, she refused to be with any of them. One of her children's fathers was having an affair with another woman, so she left him.

Furthermore, Ruth Sidles mentions the cause of women and children in poverty. *"What does it mean to a battered wife in Maine who is afraid to leave her husband because she knows she cannot possibly support their children herself."* (Sidel, 6). Women sacrifice to stay in a marriage even though it is a struggle because they know that it will be hard for them to support their children alone. *"In 1984 single parent families, 89 percent of which were headed by women. The study indicates that women are far more affected by changes in family compositions than men...divorce, death, marriage, birth are causes of being women in the female-headed family"* (Sidel, 16).

Sometimes in a situation where women need someone to talk to, she selects a man that will respect her and validate her opinion. *"He tells me he wants to marry me I look at him and think this man will not do for me. He seems like an actor just to go about on stage I like men who can do something around the house"* (St Clair, 117). As a woman why do we need men in our lives? *"...woman's physical structure and the performance of maternal functions place her at a disadvantage in the struggle for subsistence..."* (Sidel, 52).

Is this why God created men and women in this world: to work together and help each other's weaknesses and strengths? What did God plan for humanity? Did it happen? Instead, the opposite occurred. So, if we have single mothers and female-headed families, we unconsciously say, "This too shall pass," regarding the feeling of hunger. Is it a matter of choice not to get hungry? It could make you lose consciousness. Is it a decision to make to avoid hunger? Hunger can cause dizziness, fainting, and stomach pain. For women and children in poverty, how can they avoid hunger?

In conclusion, Carolina Maria de Jesus takes care of her three children by herself. Despite her struggles, she was never a bitter woman. She didn't seek the fame that found her; instead, she prayed for peace and God's protection. We should be thankful for what we have here on earth. Carolina Maria De Jesus's experiences are an example for us to learn how to strive to live without going hungry. Sir Winston Churchill says: *"a person's pessimist sees the difficulty in every opportunity, and optimist sees the opportunity in every difficulty."* Carolina Maria de Jesus found opportunity in every difficulty. She published her books and moved out of the favela after fulfilling her duty on earth. In 1977, she passed away, but her legacy is still remembered today. Her words and experiences remain in our minds, guiding us to see opportunity in every difficulty. As she said, "The woman who walks alone is likely to find herself in places no one has ever been before (Leaven 163)."

Again, is No Sex Before Marriage worth it? What is our mind and heart that matters? Also, some of this type of lifestyle, like hunger and famine today are now able to get money from the government. It is now the style and practices of single mother and take advantage of what's out there have given. Single parents or poor and hunger taking advantage of what's out there given will lose their ability to seek and create to become productive to fulfill life to the fullest.

### **Gemelya's Life Story:**

While growing up, Gemelya was discouraged by her life due to her parents' poverty and having seven siblings, two boys, and five girls. The fourth sibling passed away at age 11 due to disease, leaving only six siblings remaining. Despite the hardships of life, she learned how to survive. As a child in elementary school, she learned to sell various items such as bananas, chips, peanuts, ice candy, cheesecake, and many others to earn income, starting from first grade. The rest of her income from selling merchandise was given to her parents to buy food.

Most of Gemelya's older sisters and brothers got married earlier. Therefore, due to her hard work, she became the breadwinner of the family. Although she was very young, her interests in moving forward to achieve her goals persisted despite struggles. She became goal-oriented and kept moving forward. For example, even at a young age, Gemelya excelled academically and in sports. In high school, she was awarded as a Salutatorian and became a National Player in sports such as Table Tennis, gaining popularity in various sports, including basketball. Her favorite sport was Table Tennis, and invitations for her to attend and participate kept pouring in, including from locations like Cebu.

After high school, she worked due to hardships in life. However, it lasted for only six months as her goal was to continue her education. Therefore, she worked during the daytime and went to school at night. She chose English subjects because they were cheaper than other courses such as law. Additionally, her grades were the highest among all.

After completing several courses, she found a man and had a relationship with him. Therefore, at age 20, she got pregnant. They got married in court; however, the marriage quickly fell into disarray due to fights and arguments, primarily because the man she married chose a lazy lifestyle. The disagreements continued, with both sets of parents blaming each other for the hasty marriage without proper consideration.

It was too fast to get married without knowing each other well. Gemelya didn't continue her education, which was regrettable considering she was the brightest among students. Instead, her focus in life became taking care of her children and being a married person. Her parents criticized her for being bright in school but "too dumb" in life for choosing a man who wasn't a good husband. Consequently, Gemelya's life started to spiral into chaos, marked by more struggles and hardships. One morning, her mother suggested to her husband to find a good job because Gemelya was pregnant again with her second child. It was August 11, 2003, a year after her daughter's birthday.

Her mother was giving suggestions to her husband to find a good job because Gemelya was pregnant again with their second child. She was carrying her second child that year. When she went to her uncle's residence, they told her that he had come to ask for money. He planned to go to another city far away, Cagayan City. While she was pregnant and soon to have her second baby, she felt embarrassed because having two babies without a father seemed to ruin her reputation in the community. Despite carrying her child and their belongings while searching for her husband, she couldn't find him in Cagayan. Feeling unable to locate him, she decided to return home with her child, awaiting the arrival of her second baby. Her second baby was born on August 21, almost the same date as her eldest daughter's birthday on August 22nd.

Gemelya's oldest daughter was now a year old, and she was carrying her second child for a month. Her husband told her that he would go back to his parents to buy some milk for their child, but he did not return. She worried about having a baby without her husband and was anxious about his whereabouts. Following him to his parents' house with her year-old daughter, she found that her husband and his belongings were gone. Gemelya and her parents were worried.

Returning to her hometown without her husband, Gemelya felt that his parents were keeping secrets from her. After a week of his absence, she visited other relatives of her husband in another town and learned that he had asked for money from them to leave town, heading to faraway places like Cagayan. Upon returning home without finding her husband, she experienced frustration and distress, facing the challenges of raising her children alone.

Gemelya was very embarrassed to all her friends and relatives due to her situation as a wife without a husband with two children in hand. She was distraught, adding to shame and problems it seemed she could not figure out the solutions at that moment of her life. She was thinking about ending her life, but her common sense kept in mind that having 2 children ending life is not a good solution to the problems she was in. There were many questions in her mind about who is going to take care of her children when if she passed away. Then, she would blame herself why she got married with this irresponsible man. But it's too late it was done. She then looks back on all the opportunities in her life that she left behind.

Then Gemelya would go through a very devastating life to encounter such hunger and famine with her two children. She would cry again, and sometimes she thought of killing herself is the answer of the issues in her life. She then realized that she must find a job to earn income to buy food for her children and milk for her newborn baby. Finally, she did find a job in a factory cleaning and sanding furniture. The sanding furniture was dusty, and dust piled up in your lungs. It also creates itches in your throat and skin. However, Gemelya must work to earn income to provide necessities for her two young children. Although the salary was not enough to buy milk therefore, she must breast feed her daughter. She must go back to breast feed, and back and forth to work.

One day, she must go back to her hometown to visit her children. She plans to get another job to earn more income. She must bring her mother who was taking care of her children near where she works. Although she works overtime more often, the salary was not sufficient to buy food for her 2 children. Applying for another job has many unnecessary qualifications such as height and stature. She was busy seeking a job for a higher salary enough to support her two children. She then went back to Cebu. She walked and walked to find jobs, and she fainted almost due to too much walking, and she felt like she is going to get sick. Her knee was shaking but she kept walking and walking to find a job. Despite her struggles in seeking jobs, she never tells anyone.

Seven months past, her husband's grandparents told her to bring the children to their household. They will take care of the children and the father must be involved with the children; the grandparents promised Gemelya. She believes and trust the grandparents of her husband, and she brought the children to his grandparent's household, her mother will be able to rest of taking care of her children. The agreement was that she would be working and continue working while her husband would be the one to take care of their children. This arrangement was made by the grandparents of her husband. Through ship traveling Gemelya, her children, and her mother finally landed in Cagayan, and the husband and his grandparents were there to help them carry the luggage and the children.

Traveling from the ship to his grandparents' house took us 1 to 2 hours, in her mind she already prepares for what needs to be done and her decision is ready for her so-called husband. She decided not to have a relationship with her husband, and he would only take care of their children while she is working. She does not want to continue the husband-and-wife relationship. Due to her situation, she has to leave her children with her husband temporarily while she is working.

Although his grandparents advised them to reconcile and adopt a forgive-and-forget approach to their relationship, Gemelya was done and refused to have a relationship with her husband. Instead, she decided that her husband would take care of their children while she worked to earn an income. While they were talking and reminiscing about the past and the present, the uncle and grandparents revealed her husband's activities: he had impregnated another woman in the area and stolen his uncle's jewelry collection.

Upon learning about her husband's actions, Gemelya was distraught and decided that he would not be allowed near their children. Instead, she, along with her mother and children, moved to

Davao to settle down in that area while visiting her mom's relatives. She took on the responsibility of caring for her children without her husband's help for years. This incident led her to make the final decision not to reconcile with her husband and to keep their children away from him.

Gemelya was stunned by her husband's behavior and activities, such as stealing jewelry and impregnating another woman. She did not agree for her children to be cared for by her husband's grandparents either, especially after discovering her husband's actions. Despite the grandparents' invitation for her to stay with them and their promise to help care for the children, Gemelya hesitated, concerned about the safety and well-being of her children considering her husband's actions.

Gemelva's mother would stop by her relatives' house when they were in Davao, which was one reason she didn't agree with the grandparents' decision to care for the children. Despite not having any cash to return to her hometown, she sought help from her parents' relatives to obtain the necessary funds.

Eventually, she managed to save enough money and returned to their hometown with her children. However, upon returning, she found herself facing the same situation of hunger and famine. Overwhelmed, she cried out to the Lord for guidance. In that moment, she resolved to return to Davao, leaving her children in the care of her mother. Despite her mother's poor health, Gemelva had no choice but to find a job to survive and provide food to eat, with her parents being her only option for childcare.

While searching for a job, she encountered a student in the area who was looking for someone to help on her parents' farm. Desperate for employment, Gemelya accepted the offer and went with the student to their mango farm. The farm spanned more than a hectare, and Gemelya was introduced to a Bahay Kubo-style living space, with a roof made of dried grass and walls made of bamboo. Situated in the middle of the mango farm, the Bahay Kubo was surrounded by tall grass and far from neighbors. At night, she felt afraid and cold in the secluded Bahay Kubo, with only a towel for a blanket. Shivering in fear throughout the night, she prayed for solace in a place so distant and isolated from others.

Due to her need to feed her children, Gemelya decided to stay and pray, hoping to receive a salary for working cutting the grass on more than 4 hectares of land. However, she had to prepare herself for potential danger in the area, keeping a knife and a rosary by her side and remaining vigilant of her surroundings. With no provision of food, she had to harvest fruits to eat, relying on bananas and leaves of sweet potatoes. To cook, she made a stove out of dry branches of trees.

Gemelya reached a breaking point with her situation—

hunger, cold nights, and uncomfortable living conditions—and contemplated ending her life with the rope she had available. However, the thought of her two children relying on her postponed this decision. Still, whenever she saw the rope and tools, she couldn't help but think of ending her life. She turned to prayer, crying out to the Lord to release her from this suffering in the middle of the mango farm without food, water, or a comfortable place to rest after cleaning the farm for this family.

Finally, the harvest season arrived, bringing joy as the mango trees fruited abundantly. Gemelya eagerly anticipated receiving her salary for taking care of the mango farm for the student's family. With the harvest, she and others were hired to the mango fruits to sell in the market. The farm owner had a bountiful harvest, categorizing the fruits into first, second, and third-class types for sale. Gemelya was delighted with the successful harvest of the mango trees, bringing a sense of relief and hope for better days ahead.

After the harvesting, she got her salary, and she asked the farm owner to give her a ride home. The salary the farm owner gave her was very little, not enough to go back to her hometown. She was very shocked of the salary given. To save the money for her 2 children she asks for a ride, but the farm owner gave her a ride at the boat ride area only. The farm owner gave her a little salary, and a basket of mangoes. Therefore, Gemelya must sell the basket of mangoes added to what she given as a salary for taking care of mango farm for this family. To go back home such as paying the bus ticket and Ocean jet her money was not enough going back to her hometown.

Gemelya was very devastated of the result of her work that she didn't get the salary that she supposed to have for how many months she was working in this farm without food, not provided with blankets, and not provided with her needs to survive at the middle of the farm living in a shack. As a poor individual seeking a job to survive, she felt discriminated against and taken advantage of by the farm owners who she worked for. She insists on leaving and going back to her children with almost no money to bring to her family. The salary that the farm owner had given was just not enough to pay for the ride to her hometown. Selling the basket of mango given by the farm owner sold and she bought food for her to eat that day. The travel to her hometown takes four hours and the wait period the food she ate hopefully enough for her to survive while traveling heading back to her hometown.

Months passed by Gemelya rested she decided to wash clothes in the nearby well. Suddenly, she must stand up to get some water to drink and she fainted. Her parents were trying to help her and brought her inside. The parents called a doctor to find out what's going on with her health. She was bleeding and she suffered body exhaustion due to too much work at the mango farm. The medication was still in a traditional form such as drinking leafy vegetables of sweet potatoes that according to the local quack doctor (a traditional type of medicinal advisor but no education as a physician). It somehow works drinking sweet potato leafy soup. The parents were praying about Gemelya's situation. However, she was worried about her parents while taking care of her and taking care of her children could be too much for her parents. She prays that she will be cured as soon as possible to take over taking care of her children from her parents.

Months and months passed by her plan is to go abroad. The salary in the country is low so that income is not able to support a family of five. Therefore, her mother was helping her to find someone to help her to find an employer in Singapore. In the process of traveling leaving her children, she cried due to already missing her children. Despite missing her children, she must have a plan to survive in this world of plenty. To earn sufficient income going abroad is maybe the solution. While in the airplane, Gemelya was so surprised by the privileges in the airplane such as food given for free.

In the beginning Gemelya was worried because she did not have money to pay for the food in the airplane. This is her first travel experience outside her country. She looked at the food, it was so delicious, and she worried because she did not have money to pay for the food she had given in the airplane. She was about to refuse the food given by the stewardess. Although she accepted the food but so reluctant because she thought she must pay for the food. The stewards asked if she likes chicken and she nodded. Everybody was eating in the airplane, and she was still staring at the food given. In her thinking she does not have money to pay the stewardess.

When the plane landed, she was confused and did not know what to do. However, she just stares and stares at the people she would encounter in the airplane while preparing to land. At the end getting out of the plane, someone came to pick her up. She was amazed because the country she was in was so clean and beautiful. She started thinking what kind of life she is going to have in this country, Singapore. Today, Gemelya is a creative person making tables and chairs made of real wood. She has her own business and sells other products online. According to Einstein, "The woman who walks alone is likely to find herself in places no one has ever been before." (Albert Einstein Theoretical Physicist 1879-1955).

### The Synchronicity of Life Story:

One day, Jas called her art teacher, named Fey, and asked if she still offers art classes because all her businesses, Covid, was the reason her art classes offered were closed. After disastrous life Fey went to such as Covid that affected her life, and businesses due to flooding, sickness of previous husband and death, she went through many life struggles. Fey, Jas' art teacher used to live temporarily in Tallahassee near her son who is a physician in the area. Now at that moment that that she was back from Tallahassee to Bonifay, living in her Cabana in 3 acres land with lots of trees and meditation area, again, she offered art classes. Fey was trying to bring back the businesses that got closed due to Covid, flooding, sickness, and death of her previous husband.

Although the cabana was still in the process of finishing, she could not wait to reopen the business. However, she managed to set up the art class in her front yard looking forward to the view of her meditation area. In the beginning of the art class sessions, Jas and Fey were talking about men in their lives. Come to find out that Jas and Fey had a very similar story of their experiences. Both being a widow they talked about the many events as a woman living alone without a husband.

Jas' husband passed away in January 2020 due to blood clot, and Fey's husband passed away in December 2020 due to falling at the rehab center many times. Through grieving, Jas was comforted by her friend, Nel. Through grieving period, Fey was comforted by her builder who built her house after flooding in September 2020. Both men were kind and giving such as advices and comforted words that a woman would be needed specially the woman was in the process of grieving. With no friends around due to Covid, and being alone, having someone to be with a widow is very tempting to have a relationship with a man who comforts you and given you some words that are very positive, motivating, comforting, and a widow will not feel alone while in the process of grieving of lost husband.

Fey was guided by Tommy, the builder of her house that got flooded in the year 2020. Tommy would share his building expertise with Fey. Giving her advice about what needs to be done about her house and the process of all documentation. Meanwhile, in Jas' case is that Nel has given her a companionship, a friend companionship that in a way, Jas' son will have a man in his life while Jas was grieving of her husband's passing. These types of comforting recipe to a woman who was a widow is very tempting to be with a man that giving a widow a comfort, and a shield for heart ache, and in a loving way whether it is a friendship type of comforting. A man and a woman are meant to be attracted to one another once the spiritual world is communicating through kindness, humbleness, words that are motivated and moving forward. Then, temptation begins.

The loneliness, and aloneness somehow disappeared. Feeling of comforted by someone, somehow start to bloom, and intimacy developed. The feeling of intimacy of course developed between a man and a woman. Especially, there was an attraction in the beginning, and followed by spiritual connections through caring, kindness, humility, humbleness, and the feeling of there must be love in it. The feeling of love comforts you in the moment of suffering of your loss, such as the passing of your loved ones.

Jas was comforted by Nel throughout her grieving period

when her husband passed away in January 2020. Let me explain what it means by comforted. When a widow is alone and in the process of grieving, a widow needs someone nearby to comfort this widow. The story of Jas and Fey, her art teacher, was very similar. Jas and Fey would talk about these men in their lives while both are painting on canvas.

And this is how it begins when a man and a woman attracted each other sexual is the first attempt to feel that feeling of intimacy to one another. Since that a feeling of intimacy develops in this situation, then Jas and Fey think about morality situation. What does that mean by ethics and morality? Both, Jas, and Fey believe in ethical and moral in handling life issues, and therefore "No Sex Before Marriage" must be applied in both lives. Ethics and morality must be applied when this feeling of intimacy comes in within yourself. As we all know then and now generations that there are many young girls get pregnant so early or being pregnant without a husband as a father of their children it becomes a normal process. The children are fatherless, and single mothers rely on the help of the government as a single mother. This is what I called "Lawlessness of the Society." As what I called, Self-Respect has abandoned due to feeling of intimacy of one another, plus of course the celebrities who our children are in love with their activities as popular in the society, and television show.

Furthermore, both Jas and Fey are not girls anymore, but still carries the self-respect for themselves such as "no sex before marriage mentality." Both are in their Middle Ages. At the time of this synchronicity incident between Jas and Fey, Jas was in her 40s and Fey was in her 60s. It has been a practice since in the Caveman's era, and humans has been educated, and knowledgeable of consequences of their action, and therefore, we hope that we will see the difference between our action, and the consequences and its results whether positive, and or damage ourselves, then we hopefully learn a lesson to have self-respect, morality, ethics, and God's given power for every humans here on earth of plenty, the good common sense, wisdom, and good consciences. These are what we should ingrain within our hearts and minds.

# CHAPTER 8

# Examples of Men's Short Stories Across Cultures

Women and men expected to have roles in the society during 1800 and before. Men's roles were defined and expected to be fulfilled in the community. *"American men were presumed to be breadwinners for their families, leaders within their communities, soldiers for war and settlers of the Western frontier. Major social factors shaped the roles of men in the 1800s. These included the Industrial Revolution, slavery, Westward expansion, the railroad system, the Victorian era and various wars"* *(Bing 2023).*

First, in this generation still exist about men supposedly tough in regards heavy load of lifting and driving huge trucks. It's a manly type of responsibility, heavy loads. We as women can't do it because we are women versus men are stronger than we are as women. Men were train to be tough. They are train to be a man. What is a man by the way? Previous generation, the traditional way men were taught not to cry. Because crying is a weakness they say from the traditional era. Of course, today we have women do what men supposed to do but it is obvious men do differently than women. Men's performance as a man versus a woman specially in heavy loads, the results is different.

Men genetically develop muscles than women unable to have. Although, women today are trying to develop muscles, but women's body is unable to imitate men's body shape. Men's body shape is different than of a woman. We are structured differently as a man and a woman. As we all know that David and Goliath story as supposed to be a man-to-man fight. Humans are God's creation we can't ignore that. We can't change it and we cannot reshape it. *"Men are, in general, more muscular than women. Women are just over **half as strong** as men in their upper bodies, and about two-thirds as strong in their lower bodies. [What's the Strongest Muscle In the Human Body?] While the male metabolism burns calories faster, the female metabolism tends to convert more"* (Bing, 2024).

### **<u>Thomas' Life Story:</u>**

Since Thomas was a boy, he was trained not to cry. Thomas was also trained that a man supposedly has many concubines as the practice of people a decade ago. When he got married, he had a boy, his wife had an affair while Thomas went to work. One day, he came home from work and found his wife with a man in their bedroom. Their son was crying while his wife was having a moment of reminiscing with her lover. Thomas was devastated by his wife's activity. Therefore, he decided to divorce his wife. Immediately, he picked up his son and took him to his parents' house. Therefore, his parents were now taking care of his son.

The action of his wife makes Thomas very ashamed as he is supposedly a man. The belief since a long time ago was that a man should not cry, and a man should be strong and has many concubines. Thomas started to have many women in his life. He would attend a contest of motorcycle riding all the way up to the mountain. He then believes that conquering many obstacles, having many concubines, fast and furious types of activity make you a man within. Also, became a man of strength and belief such as he should not cry and should have lots of concubines as what the practice of people a long time ago that it brought up to his days of living here on earth.

As a writer of this book, "But, Hey, What Matter is What's In Your Heart and Mind" is not what people see you, as of who you are supposedly following the beliefs decade ago. Do not pay attention to people who are judging who you supposedly be. Create the YOU of who you want to be applying the good consciences and common sense within your thought and practices. As humans here on earth we have a Thought Universe, I call it. What's in our thought universe is very vague and much information we have gathered since when we are growing up. We must select what we must gather within our mind and shape our mind and heart with good common sense, wisdom, and good consciences. I say that it is okay for a man to cry. We all have emotions within ourselves, man or a woman because WE are humans.

Crying releases tenses within our mind and heart, unloading some cargo from the thought universe. As thought universe is vague and wide which carries all baggage we have while journey here on earth of plenty. It would not make you weak as a man when you cry. Instead, it releases pressure you hold within your heart and mind. Therefore, it cleanses the thought universe within you and then, able to load another. However, make sure you load something that is positive and uplifting to move forward. Therefore, what's in your hearts and minds matters.

### **Max's Short Story:**

When Max was a little boy he went through life without a brother, and had an abusive father, and the father died in a car accident. The mother was not available for anyone. His father was raised as of a man supposedly to be a dominance within the family. Max with 4 sisters has a broken home growing up. He was feeling isolated.

It is still a belief in the past, as male and female to be isolated as male has a privilege to be a dominance in the family unit. On the father side, without balance and without using common sense, and the issue becomes worse and to the extreme that it becomes a habit believing that man should be dominance in the family. Due to issues in the family, Max went to drinking and drugs. It took years for Max to realize the devastation in life, Max went to AA instead. Max choses the positive life, no drugs, no alcohol, and he chose to live by himself alone for 30 years being sober. Then, Max found a love of his life, a woman, name Mary who loves him so much, and Max and Mary have a great relationship together.

### Bernies' Short Story:

On the other hand, the story of Bernie that carry on the knowledge as male supposedly when sin be hanged. As we all know that men or any human beings must be hanged when you create a crime or sinning which a long time ago rules and regulations. Bernie's grandfather brought this knowledge and learned behavior. Such as when Bernie does not obey the rules, he would be punished by hanging and tie him with a rope. In those eras, it was acceptable. His grandfather carried on that belief while Bernie was a very young boy. This behavior of his grandfather affected the new generation, and therefore, Bernie would punish his children through using belts and perhaps would hang his son with a rope if the wife didn't stop him.

If no one stopped him at that moment of anger and punishment hanging a little boy as a punishment, in his mind it is suitable for the boy to become a man. Therefore, it is still within the minds of humanity on what they think a disciplinary tactic for boys to grow up as a boy to become a man. The struggles of men a long time ago while growing up carried over to these days here on earth of plenty and provided. Humans must really differentiate between eras and these days teaching and knowledge may differ in disciplining our children. Knowledge and always having good common sense, good wisdom, and good conscience must be applied towards these types of disciplinary action.

We, the parents and or foster cares who trusted to guide our children of today, must remember that the brain of a little child still in process of development. Meaning, the THOUGHT UNIVERSE of a little child still in the development stages. What that means is parents should develop their little children into a child that balances events in their lives, and always inserting the disciplinary action through kindness, humbleness, and humility. So, then a child that is developed to that direction is equip of good, positivity, and surrounded with good common sense, and good conscience.

### **Mitch's Short Story:**

Mitch's story as a boy reflected on when he was growing up and became a man. As the practices before in his era, he thoughts that having many concubines are acceptable due to until these days we are still inherited the beliefs that as a man should have many concubines. Again, learning while growing up and the people around you who were with you, a child carry what they learn while growing from a little boy to become a man. If Mitch was train by influential people around him, he would do the same as the practice of men before to have many concubines.

These practices ruin marriages, and family units. Therefore, there are so many single parents today, and pregnancy are not important anymore as to what other women using pregnancy as financial reason to collect from the government such as a child support, and or other help from the government for single parents. Also, not only ruined marriages, but this practices also ruins the growing up of the young children that today there are so many abandoned children or selling children or using parts of the body to sell to get money. Such a sad world, and the government has no answers.

Having many concubines, women to be pregnant is now a commercialized financial activity that no one or shall I say, has been ignored due to misunderstanding, and just do not care but instead relying on an individual to make decision as we think. Do they know what they are heading about this type of lifestyle? Therefore, there are many cases about human trafficking. According to sources (Google, 2024) "In United States and around the world traffickers are estimate to exploit 40.3 million victims, and with an estimated 25 million victims in forced labor and 15 million victims in forced marriage" (Google, 2024). Again, in this case the experiences of these children, victims, and the victimizers ingrained in their hearts and minds that become serious issues in our society today.

# CHAPTER 9

# Skin Color Versus Trans Disease

A fourteen-year-old girl suffers from XYY disease syndrome. Therefore, it is difficult for this fourteen-year-old who was named Skyler. Skyler was psychologically examined, after operation to trans. Skyler suffered from suicidal, depression, and tried to kill herself through cutting her wrist. She felt like a boy not a girl. "His confusion grew painfully over time. Skyler's first period, at age 11, was traumatic. Every month he would spend an entire week at home, unable to face school." The biggest challenge of this disease is psychologically, ethically, mental illness. Skyler's doctors examine this type of disease through physical health, emotional maturity, gender history, review Skyler's gender history, and other host of details regarding this disease syndrome, but the doctor's follow up was unclear (Mantenex, 2023).

According to Mantenex (2023) "there are people who suffer from XYY syndrome - one more Y. There are also cases where a male mutation has an additional Y chromosome **(XYY Syndrome - or "super-male" syndrome)**. If you think XYY has more male characteristics: more muscular, more masculine, even more aggressive. Then you're wrong. XYY is a disease syndrome, so it is difficult for patients to develop normally. A person with chromosome XYY will in fact have more female-like characteristics, weaker muscles, reduced intelligence, and slower development" (Mantenex, 2023).

### **<u>Beyond XX and XY Study:</u>**

From the moment a child is born we always distinguish whether it is a boy or a girl. We as humans are socially conditioned to view sex and gender as binary attributes to every human before and after the fetus was born. Humans are socially conditioned to view sex and gender as binary attributes. From the moment we are born—or even before—we are definitively labeled "boy" or "girl." "Yet science points to a much more ambiguous reality. Determination of biological sex is staggeringly complex, involving not only anatomy but an intricate choreography of genetic and chemical factors that unfolds over time. Intersex individuals—those for whom sexual development follows an atypical trajectory—are characterized by a diverse range of conditions, such as 5-alpha reductase deficiency" (Amanda Manexi).

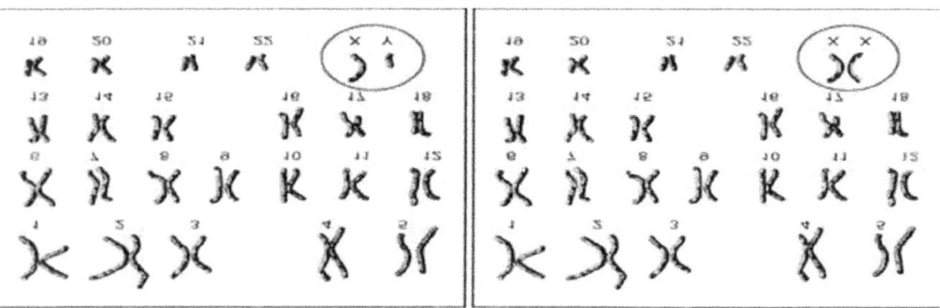

Today, scientists are busy researching in finding cure of this type of disease, the trans diseases with extra genome, either XXX or XYY. The normal genome is XX for a girl, and XY for the boy fetus. See the illustration of the genomes above of the identifier of XX for girls, and XY for boys' chromosomes.

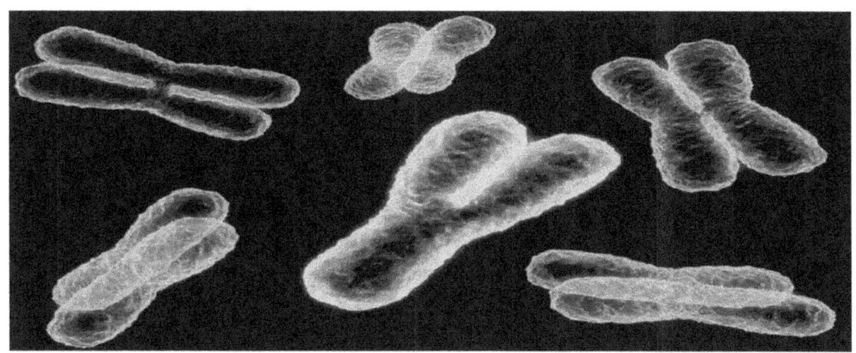

This illustration is for the people who suffer from XYY syndrome. One more Y creates trans disease. The case of male mutation with extra Y instead of XY only is a syndrome scientist called "Super-Male XYY syndrome. According to Manexi,(2023), having two YY does not mean that this boy has more characteristic as a male, but it difficult for this boy to function normally as a boy. A person with an XYY will in fact has more female-like characteristics, weaker muscles, reduced intelligence, and slower development (Manexi, 2023).

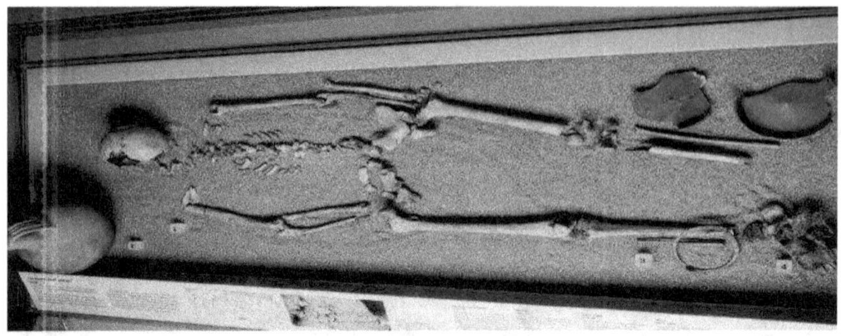

From London Museum, the photo was excavated in year 1979. The skeleton above has male chromosome. According to researcher, she lived between 50 to 70 BC. However, she died when she was at age 26 to 35 years old. The DNA was analyzed out of 20,000 skeletons to understand humanity on how they live before, and in comparison, to today and its composition.

This woman was buried in a wooden casket. Necklace was placed in the casket referring that this is a woman. A vase, and copper mirror were placed in the coffin and woman's foot. These artifacts shows that it is a woman and this woman play an important role in high status in her era. According to London Museum spokesman, this illustration from the Ancient Origins about a woman whose DNA has both X and Y chromosomes. The skeleton was found in Harper Road, in London, and was in a woman's shape. The pelvis and skull characteristics used to identify sex result in this woman found.

**A syndrome called; Androgen Insensitivity Syndrome**

**causes patients to have a female-shape but carry a male chromosome**. But according to scientists' information about the state of the ancient woman is not enough to confirm this is the causes of this strange characteristic. Although, there is no evidence of a woman's behavior or figure. My theory and question would be: was this woman imitating Nefertiti in her lifetime playing the role as a woman and a man in the society? Again, this woman was accepted and even revered by the community (Manexi, 2023, Google).

Occasionally, I would think about an idea and reasoning that make sense. Transhumanism is the experimentation of humans here on earth, I would say. Have you been experimented by the belief in changing your identity as a man to become a woman and or a woman to become a man? The transgender is just the beginning of this manipulation through confusing strategy for humans to be lost in the wild world. It is just the beginning, and the chaos is coming such as example girls are raped in the bathroom because boys now able to pretend, they are girls. Boys pretend as a transgender (because being transgender is acceptable) can get into boy or girls' restroom. What's the difference between the two? What is right and wrong practices being colored skin or transgenderism practices?

According to research lately, transgenderism is a disease, and its practice it's a lifestyle maybe chosen by individual due to some kind of mental disarray, confusion, and hallucination issues.

In addition, experimentation of humanity are the causes of these types of lifestyles. Again, XY for a boy genome became XYY then therefore it becomes a disease that this person is carrying, the trans disease called Androgen Insensitivity Syndrome. It is now in the process for finding a medication for this type of disease, the trans disease. Developing a medicine for this disease is currently unknown.

How about skin color, may I ask? Can you change your DNA for your skin from dark to white or white to dark skin? Can you change the color of your skin? No. Unless you have some chemical to change your color from dark to white or vice versa. Again, these chemicals are humans' creation to whiten the skin, or sunbathing under the sun for the skin to be tan color.

Is a boy able to change his male organ to become a female organ? Yes, through human's creation of believing that these humans think they are the GOD of the universe. Operation to remove a male organ to make it into a female organ also happening in our world today. Of course, there will be consequences of these actions by these individuals when the time comes. Again, XY is a boy and XX is a girl. Other than that, it becomes a disease as XXX or XYY or vice versa. A disease must be cured or else there will be consequences. However, not to a point removing a male organ to change it to a female organ or vice versa, it is not a cure for trans disease.

Thus, it is not a cure to change sex organ to another of what you think, I said, what you think who you are as how you FEEL who you are such a feeling of like a girl or like a boy, but it is through removing extra genes is the cure. Scientists are still in the process of researching on how to remove the extra genome from your chromosome such if XXX or XYY within you, then currently the study to find cure for this trans disease is ongoing. How do you remove extra Y or X within a human being? It is now in the process to find for a cure for this type of disease, the trans disease (Manexi, 2023).

Albert Einstein says, "The world is a dangerous place to live, not because of the people who are evil, but because of the people who don't do anything about it" (Einstein, 1879-1955). Similar to my question as why does society accept gender manipulation practice and lifestyle? Why is society always against, or shall I say, questionnaires always have a question of what skin color you have? The question would be why society does not accept skin color and it seems being black, white, red, yellow, and brown is not accepted but gender manipulation is favored and accepted in society? I am so sorry to say that society, or shall I say we, as HUMANS, are so naïve, unable to use our common sense provided by our Almighty.

The practices and lifestyles of such transgenderism, the trans disease practices should not be accepted, however, it is now accepted such as manipulation of XY a male, and XX a female chromosome a sex determination of such a born child. In comparison to a DNA results of skin colored individual is not accepted in the society because of the colored skin. Skin colors are based on the DNA or RNA of an individual. XYY and or XXX with an extra chromosome hanging on the regular chromosomes of XX and or XY should be removed. A person has the right to be normal by having only XX and XY chromosomes, NOT 3 or 4 chromosomes. A person with a disease that an extra X or Y, the trans disease must be removed from the person to be normal and avoiding mutilating the sexual organ of an individual.

It depends on your culture and who your parents and grandparents are. What's in the mind of an individual and the influences surrounding our children of today are also the reasons why our children are lost in this era, and unable to distinguish between right and wrong. We may ask, what is the content of your mind, which I called the Thought Universe?

Knowing What's in the Heart and the Mind is an important activity for all humans. Do we pay attention to what is in our heart and mind? Or are we ingrained in numbing it due to confusion and many activities in this world of good and evil? We always have desires in our heart. The difference between our desires is the question of what type of desires you developed within your heart and mind? What we develop in the mind is unseen world activity of humanity. Unless that unseen event is visually acted through explanation or body language then an individual can be understood or perhaps misunderstood if coordination is not match.

Through body language an example is hallucination and when action is taken therefore you can see or hear only what has been hallucinated upon. We as humans uses words that would either live or kill an individual or yourself therefore knowledge of words usage must be examined first before releasing it to someone and or to yourself.

Examining what's in your heart and mind is like cleansing your vast containers of spiritual body, the unseen of humanity's being. Therefore, we heard the words, wisdom, consciences, and common senses. The questions would be these the GOOD wisdom, consciences, and common senses? Based on what you gather in your heart and mind that will become YOU is your choice in life. Therefore, many that good wisdom, conscience, and common senses are seared and or smeared due to struggle and bad experiences in life since a child growing up.

However, the power of Self will always be able to reverse bad experiences and the struggles as tools to gear life bad experiences as learning process and use your power to build good wisdom, consciences, and common senses, and it is possible. There are many ways on how to bring back your life to powerful self. Becoming productive and creative and of course prayers help us to realign our wishes and form our good wisdom, good consciousness, and good common senses for a healthy heart and mind.

Let us give a few examples of what the contents within our Thought Universe are. Through Fine Art Formation Abstract forms of art have no definite lines and shapes such as the Thought Universe is an art that plays colors, and every color has meaning. Knowledgeable educated artists know the meaning of colors in an abstract and realistic form. For example, the Physic Universe such as a landscape art the formation is mixed.

In landscape artwork, the far away image is not that clear in the painting. Once we see the far image closer, we can only imagine what it is. The closer the landscape is the visibility is good. In similarity to The Two Universes of Self also has these types of visibility and non-visibility. The Physic as a visibility form, and the Thought has non visibility form but the only way we will be able to see is to only imagine and through words of communication. Once visualization is formed through imagination within our mind then it is clear who you tried to form who you are and what you are going to become.

For clarification, you must repeat, bring back memories, repaint it over, recycle it, reform it, become a habit, be addicted to it, and it will become YOU once you use these visualization processes. In a way, it is probably benefiting if we have a forgetful mind not to remember previous hurtful and self-damaging events in your life. Instead, be selective and start a new YOU, a new you with positive, productive, and creative Self that are good for the Physic and the Thought Universes. Last sentence I would like to say, that if you want to fight back use good common sense, good conscience, and good wisdom, and you always win the battle in spiritual and earthly world. What's in our mind and heart is what matters the most.

# IN CONCLUSION

Whether your skin color is white, brown, yellow, or black, it does not matter. What's matter is of who we are within us the content of our hearts and minds as an individual person, not by skin color. Also, for us to move forward in our life pursuit and lifestyle we must choose what's right in our journey in life. We are just temporary here on earth of plenty and we so free, but there are so many choices living in this world we must make sure that we chose the right direction with God's guidance and be thankful for all blessings we received every day.

We are the children of God, and we are in many different skin colors that it meant to be. However, the lifestyle and practices that ruins humans is not from God's intention, but it is human's intentions such as Transgenderism lifestyle and practices. As we always say to self-respect, we must seek what's right and move forward in line on what we are supposed to be as the Lord has already given for all humanity. Listening to Dolly Parton's song titled *"Coats Of Many Color"* has given me a meaningful message that humans are in "Coats Of Many Color. *"Why Can't We Live Together"* by Sade is song that is meaningful to a point where each every one of us since Covid lived in isolation.

Not only that the culture and skin color discrimination in the country become so obvious and wide open, but it is still not acceptable. On the other side, we also turn on our mentality that everyone should be accepted such as transgenderism, the disease now scientist found, and looking and searching for cure at the time this manuscript was in the writing process.

This disease scientist finding of a syndrome called **Androgen Insensitivity Syndrome** causes patients to **have a female shape but carry a male chromosome**. "But according to scientists, information about the state of the ancient woman is not enough to confirm this is the cause of this strange characteristic. Although there is no evidence of a woman's behavior or figure, from burial items in the grave, the girl is accepted and even revered by the community. Because of ethical, psychological, mental confusion due to feeling of whether a boy or a girl that no one knows the answer yet, but only the finding of Androgen Insensitivity Syndrome carried by male or female chromosomes, it is a disease that needs attention, create solution, and finding the cure of this type of diseased, the trans disease. Again, good common sense, consciences, and wisdom the God given skills and tools are now lost from within us as humans, God's children here on earth of plenty. My question would as if parents taking drugs while pregnant created Androgen Insensitivity Syndrome that ruins the fetus from the beginning. There are so many questions how this happened, a trans disease that ruins our children of today, and tomorrows to come.

Again, what's in your mind and heart matters, not the color

of your skin, and the practices and lifestyles that will ruin your spiritual world, and your physical world which I called The Two Universes of Self, the thought, and the physic universes within the self. The big question would be since that it is accepted in the society, the trans disease, is this drug experimentation process, and the popularity of media attention about this trans disease through celebrities influences our children of today, the acceptance of it the cure may not be processed due to how they feel within as a boy with a feeling of like a girl, and a girl feeling with a feeling like a boy is immorally accepted these days.

A boy with a male organ XY chromosome, and a girl with a female organ XX chromosome continually be a normal individual? Is the cure for this trans disease to remove extra chromosome such as XXX and XYY can be processed? The ongoing process these days is boys and girls mutilated their bodies through cutting and installing private organs due to their feelings, felt like a girl or a boy which we are all have those due to our emotions. Emotions are within all of us as humans, whether you are a boy or a girl. Such as it is okay to cry if you are a man, and if you are a girl, it's okay to lift heavy things because of our capabilities within us. It does not mean that men cannot cry, and women cannot lift up heavy things, common sense must be applied.

Again, I would say, what's in your mind and heart is what matters because feelings are what you have in your mind. This feeling can be altered as what you are supposedly and physically. Meaning, if you have a male organ then you are a boy or a man, and if you are a female, if you have a female organ then you are a girl or a woman. Try this if you feel like crying, and you saw someone laughing, how do you feel? Also, if you feel like your skin is too white and change that skin color into tan, you would be under the sun, right? Or you may put tanning lotion on your skin. If you have a tan color skin wants to have a white skin, would you like to put some chemical or lotion with whitening chemical to have a white skin? Therefore, "But, Hey! What Matters Is What You Have in Your Mind and Heart."

# Wisdom In Every Situation

(From book titled "Be Still And Know" (Copyright to Broadstreet Publishing Group, LLC)

Then you will understand what is right, just, and fair, and you will find the right way to go. For wisdom will enter your heart, and knowledge will fill you with joy. Wise choices will watch over you. Understanding will keep you safe (Proverbs 2:9-11 NLT).

All of life is a test. As we live each day, the tests we face teach us valuable lessons. It may seem backwards: usually lessons are learned to prepare us for a test. But in life, the test often comes first. Through the lessons, God gives us the wisdom we need for the next test.

It's a safe bet that the tests will keep coming. Thankfully, our hearts gain understanding every time. Tension and uncertainty melt away, job blossoms. Solomon's advice is that we listen to wisdom, apply it, and learn as we go. Then we will have understanding; we will find the right path with wisdom in our hearts and joy from knowledge.

God, you have taught me so many valuable lessons from life's tests. I take joy in the wisdom I have gained from those tests. Thank you for giving me the opportunity to make wise choices. (Broadstreet Publishing, 2016, page 383).

# Albert Einstein

(Theoretical Physicist 1879-1955)

*"The world is a dangerous place to live, not because of the people who are evil, but because of the people who don't do anything about it."*

*"If you want to live a happy life, tie it to a goal, not to people or things."*

*"The woman who walks alone is likely to find herself in places no one has ever been before."*

**THE END.**

# About The Author

## Dr. Sofia Laurden-Davis Adams

Sofia Laurden-Davis Adams is a PhD in Human Services specialized in Management in Nonprofit Agencies and Leadership graduated in April 2014 at Capella University. Dr. Adams is currently an Independent Contractor with mortgage, bank, law, and title companies function as a Certified Signing Specialist. Dr. Adams was born in Bohol Island Philippines. She came to United States in year 1984. She has 2 sons, Rhoss (Junjun) 41, and Danny (Jr) 34 years of age. Both sons are married, and currently she has six grandchildren. Danny is a medical doctor, and Rhoss is in logistics.

Since 1989, Dr. Sofia Laurden-Davis Adams worked in banking and real estate industries. At the beginning of the year 2000, she became an Independent Contractor working part time while pursuing her education. Currently, she is an entrepreneur, a volunteer of Guardian Ad Litem, serving as the voice for neglected and abused children in three counties in Panhandle Florida. and she taught 4th & 5th religious education in the church she attended. She teaches art classes and offers "Courtesy Art Classes" and she travels to art students' selected location, and class can be held in her own Fine Art Studio. She is an Independent Contractor performing signings for mortgage, bank, and title companies.

Dr. Adams graduated as a Doctor of Philosophy (PhD) in April 2014. In 2006 she graduated with a master's degree in human resource management from the University of Phoenix. She has a bachelor's degree major in Art History, and Studio Art at Georgian Court University in New Jersey graduated in 2004, and an associate degree in liberal arts doubled with Photography at Brookdale Community College graduated in 2000. She moved from Bricktown, New Jersey to Bonifay Florida in 2004.

The same year, she developed a 501 C3 organization named Bonifay Guild for the Arts, Inc. which in year 2010 this organization was renamed to Laurden-Davis & Associates sole proprietorship consists of Mobile Signing Agent, Notary Public, Fine Art Studio, Online Art Gallery, and Rental Properties. Dr. Adams developed a yearbook for her previous organization titled, "Memorable Moments of Bonifay Guild for the Arts, Inc. Part 1" The book has 110 pages of compiled photos, stories, and activities of Bonifay Guild for the Arts, Inc. The yearbook copies were placed at Chambers of Commerce, and libraries for previous BGA and LDA members' keepsakes.

Dr. Sofia Laurden-Davis Adams and her husband Cameron plan to travel internationally. She plans to continue writing books and curricula, and as an independent contractor function as art teacher, Certified Signing Specialist. Dr. Adams published her books since year 2014 to this day. Check her books below:

www. authordrsofiaadams.com

www.amazon.com

www.ingramSpark.com

www.drsofiaadams.com

www.xlibris.com

www.iUniverse.com

www.morebooks.de

www.cameron-adams.com (and her husband Cameron is also an artist doing wood artworks.